Ruth Artmonsky

TUPPENCE PLAIN
Penny Coloured

Fifty years of furniture advertising and selling

Published by:
Artmonsky Arts
Flat 1, 27 Henrietta Street
London WC2E 8NA
www.ruthartmonsky.com
artmonskyruth@gmail.com
Tel. 020 7240 8774

Text © Ruth Artmonsky 2016
ISBN 978-0-9935878-0-1

Designed by:
David Preston Studio
www.davidprestonstudio.com

Printed in England by:
Northend Creative Print Solutions
www.northend.co.uk

Acknowledgements:
My thanks go to Stella Harpley, the
best of researchers; to the staff in
the archives of the Geffrye Museum;
to my fellow ephemera enthusiasts
Leonie Highton, Robin Wyatt and
Brian Webb who generously lent
material; and, as always, to David
and Tamsin Preston, my original and
conscientious book designers.

Contents

Opposite page: Undated illustration for Harris Lebus furniture catalogue.
Previous spread: Cover of Smarts furniture catalogue, undated.

Introduction

The title of this book – *Tuppence Plain, Penny Coloured* is borrowed from a published speech given to the Royal Society of Arts in 1950, by the then Professor of Wood, Metals and Plastics at the Royal College of Art. Prof. R.D. Russell (Dick), and his brother Gordon, were both designers for the family firm, Gordon Russell Ltd., which was to set the par when it came to design and production standards for 20th century British furniture. In four words – 'Tuppence Plain, Penny Coloured' Dick Russell was able to sum up the battle confronting the industry – on the one side a handful of designers, manufacturers and retailers, supported by the Design & Industries Association and by the Council for Art & Industry (that was resurrected post-WWII as the Council of Industrial Design); on the other was the bulk of the British furniture industry and, indeed, the bulk of British furniture buyers. The issue at stake was a matter of honesty and quality – simple, well-designed, functional furniture, made from good materials by crafts people using appropriate machinery (consequently pricey) versus shoddy, often 'period' repro furniture, mass-produced using cheap materials, decorated to cover up poor construction and 'pushed' by retailers at cut-prices, tempting by hire purchase a gullible public.

Let's face it, furniture is not the easiest thing to sell however constructed or designed. Food and drink need to be bought weekly, if not daily; household products monthly; clothes with seasonal fashion changes. But furniture is only bought a few times in anyone's life – when starting a home or when moving house. And furniture is relatively expensive, likely to take up a considerable portion of an annual income, and not likely to be bought on impulse.

And further, furniture is not the easiest thing to show to attract potential customers, being, until the years post-Festival of Britain and post the introduction of plastics, largely brownish in colour, largely lacking such qualities as the cache of, say, the motor car, or the sex appeal of fashion and make-up. It is not insignificant that some fifty years of the trade magazine *Display* rarely carried an example of good practice when it came to furniture display. It is, perhaps, paradoxical that some of the best 20th century designers were attracted to designing furniture, producing iconic pieces now displayed in museums, yet as a product it has only occasionally attracted the talents of the display designer. And as far as graphic design is concerned, whether for furniture catalogues or press advertisements, it has generally been branded run-of-the-mill stuff, or worse, and has certainly fallen below the radar of most graphic design historians and critics. This book is an attempt to show the many different ways furniture manufacturers and retailers have actually handled the 'showing off' of their wares, warts and all; an account that has found some surprisingly good examples, whether the furniture being hyped was tuppence plain or penny coloured.

*The atmosphere in which you buy
something is as important in influencing sales
as the nature and price of a product.*

Penny Sparke, *Did Britain Make It?*

'Buildings' – the siting of a shop, store, emporium, its size, its frontage, its internal layout, were all contributory factors to the selling of furniture. It was as if furniture companies were declaiming 'This is how we see ourselves and want to be seen; what you see on the outside reflects the character of what is to be seen inside'. Whether the furniture was being sold from the East or West Ends, the message was 'this is what we are about'.

C. Edwards, in a Loughborough University paper, starts with a significant paragraph, albeit probably indecipherable by the common reader –

Over the last sixty years, the four fundamentals of central place theory, spatial interaction, the principle of minimal differentiation and bid-rent theory have underpinned much analysis of clustering and business location, especially in the retail sector.

What this boils down to is that birds of a feather, for a number of different reasons, flock together, as Savile Row found useful with tailoring and Cork Street with art. When it came to furniture selling, at least as far as London was concerned, 'clustering' occurred in two broad areas – the

East End, generally characterized as selling cheap tawdry wares, and the West End selling high quality craftsmen built furniture – after all Chippendale had had his workshop on St. Martin's Lane.

The clustering in the East End had largely come about because of the transport advantages of the canal and the London docks for timber, and the increasing availability of cheap labour with the waves of immigration, particularly Jewish, in the 19th century. A key player, for example, was the arrival of the Lebus family, setting up in a modest way in the East End, but by the beginning of the 20th century, having moved out to Tottenham, claiming to be the largest cabinet maker in the United Kingdom.

In the East End, Curtain Road has been described as the 'nerve centre' of the industry; the London Street Directory for 1921 listed more than fifty establishments in Curtain Road in the furniture trade or linked to it. Although early furniture selling may have been no more than putting pieces outside the workshop (which also served as a home and a lodging for the apprentice), by the mid-19th

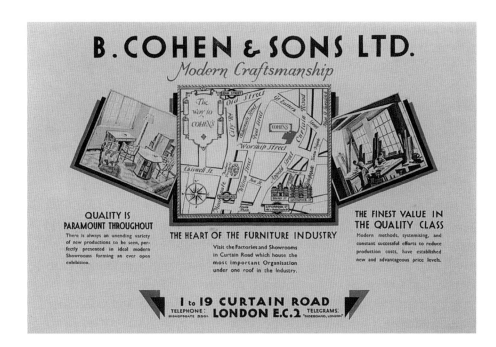

century much of the East End furniture selling took place from wholesale warehouses, with grand frontages stretching along the surrounding streets, each warehouse covering several floors. In *Behind the Veneer* the authors describe the spread –

> In Curtain Road, from Old Street to Great Eastern Street, at one time, every shop save four was a wholesale furniture warehouse. Into Great Eastern Street, Rivington Street, Worship Street, City Road, Old Street, Scrutton Street, Tabernacle Street, and all the interesting streets of that district wholesale emporiums seem to have been spilled. At any time during the week from the purloins of Hoxton, from Old Ford, Bethnal Green and the byways of Shoreditch could be seen vans and weird piles of furniture in unpolished or skeletal form.

These grand showrooms usually consisted of a basement for packing and distribution, and some three floors of showrooms, often with the

supporting cast iron columns, the supports of the building, being left unadorned. Even by the 1920s, by which time many of the East End manufacturers were selling directly to retailers and the wholesale warehouses had declined, there were still over two hundred furniture workshops around Kingsland Road, Hackney Road, and the adjoining streets.

Parallel to what was going on in the East End of London, the furniture trade was growing in the West End, aided by a rapidly developing transport system of buses, trams, trains and the underground, and by the introduction of street lighting, which was well established in Tottenham Court Road early in the 19th century. This area, being central, was altogether more easily accessible for potential customers. As Curtain Road was the nerve centre for the East End firms, so Tottenham Court Road and its surrounding streets became the magnet for much of the West End. As Hoxton, Hackney and Shoreditch were to contain much of the East End furniture industry, so the borough of Camden, stretching as it does to Holborn and Oxford Street, had Bowmans at the northern end, Drage to the east on High Holborn, Waring & Gillow and the

Below: Shops with workshops at the rear, Worship Street. **Bottom:** Tabernacle Street – where Harris Lebus moved to in 1885. **Right:** Loading gear on the front of a Leonard Street furniture warehouse.

Times Furnishing Co. on New Oxford Street with Hampton's and Bolsom's just south of the area, near Trafalgar Square. Tottenham Court Road, itself, was to be crowded with the likes of Maples, Heal's, Shoolbred, Catesby's, and Wolfe & Hollander, with Oetzmann's nearby on Hampstead Road.

Many of the West End furniture stores had started as small shops, or shops and workshops, Maples and Shoolbred selling drapery, Heal's known for its bedding. Gradually they began to acquire neighbouring properties and soon the higgledy-piggledy of buildings began to morph, with the need for consolidation, into grand emporia, with impressive façades. Maples, which had started at no. 145 in 1841, by the early years of the 20th century extended along Tottenham Court Road, Tottenham Place and Southampton Court to the Euston Rd, and had become as much a tourist attraction as Harrods. It had actually started sometimes selling its goods on the pavement outside its small frontage, but, by the 1920s, extended over some forty acres with a car park for customers. In the 1930s it was given an even more splendid façade described as –

Opposite page: Warings retail premises, Oxford Circus, complete with sign: 'Take a walk around Warings – the most beautiful shop in London'.

Below: Gordon Russell's 17th century showrooms and workshops added in 1919, Broadway, Worcestershire.

Above: Heal's, Tottenham Court Road, 1920s.
Opposite page: Typical 1930s out-of-London furniture store, Wolfe & Hollander, Bromley.

classic in conception with a colonnade of beautifully proportioned columns crowned with composite capitols, the general effect is both impressive and traditional.

Maples was to be badly bombed in 1940–1, the rebuilding not really started until 1950, with the shop not fully reopened until 1959. The destruction of its building somehow symbolized what was happening to the company. By 1972 the premises were demolished and redeveloped, and Maples was to concentrate in the future on developing its chain of stores.

Whereas Maples's grand building had become a rendezvous for the rich and fashionable, the building, furniture and clients all in tune, Heal's architecture was to send out a rather different message. It is true that its early façade, by J. Morant Lockyer, was of the Italian Renaissance style with coloured pilasters and Minton tiles, but by 1916 this had been replaced. Ambrose Heal, being one of the more design-conscious furniture proprietors, had his cousin, Cecil Brewer, along with Dunbar Smith, design a near-modernist building of Portland

TO-DAY.

ESTABLISHED 1864

Above: Bowman Brothers, Camden Town. **Opposite page left:** Drage interior, 1932.
Opposite page right: Betty Joel showing at Fortnum & Mason, 1930s.

stone, with a colonnade of columns stretching
from the entrance, and with much noted features
as a decorative frieze of panels carrying images
of the various products on sale inside and, even
more remarked upon by both the architectural and
general press, large concave glass windows. When

Edward Maufe designed an extension, erected in
1937, Heal's claimed the longest stretch of non-
reflective glass at the time. In 1962 there was a
further extension, by Herbert Fitzroy Robinson,
and by then the showrooms were estimated to cover
some 11,000 square feet. Heal's was to become the

meeting place for the cultured classes, particularly after it had set up its Mansard Gallery in the 1920s. The ever caustic John Betjeman recorded –

> ...as one who takes even greater pleasure in walking around Maples and Waring and Gillows, than among the pale high-class simplicity of Heal's...

Bowmans, in Camden Town, perhaps an exception to the idea that the exterior reflecting the products, was to draw in a similar crowd to Heal's, in spite of its arts and crafts building, with Dutch gables, red brick and stonework dressing and mosaic inlays, the façade coming to bely the firm's increasingly modern furniture.

Of course, much furniture during the period of this book, was being sold in the very grand buildings of general department stores, as Harrods, Liberty, Whiteleys, the Army & Navy Stores, Selfridges, John Lewis and Peter Jones. But for these the odd shop window displaying furniture had to serve as a draw, albeit sometimes not a particularly attractive one, for the furniture floors or part-floors could well be swamped by the more glamorously displayed ones selling fashion, beauty products and food.

Perhaps some of the most interesting London furniture showrooms in the 1930s, were those set up by manufacturers based outside. Parker-Knoll, having moved out of Curtain Road to High Wycombe decided it needed a London base

and opened one in Newman Street at the turn of the 20th century. Initially this consisted of one floor, but gradually others were acquired. This enabled the firm to mount displays and to keep its considerable archive of over three thousand photos, which could be seen not only by interested retailers but by the general public. Later it decided also to set up showrooms in Manchester, Birmingham and Bristol. Shutting down during WWII Parker-

Knoll revived the idea of a London base after the war, moving it two or three times before settling in Berners Street.

It was the Cavendish Square area that attracted first Gordon Russell's and later Pel. Gordon Russell had opened his first London base in Wigmore Street. in 1929. Although the intent was that it should show just the Russell's furniture, that of Gordon and

Opposite page: Office furniture display, Peter Jones, 1950s. **Right:** Parker-Knoll display in Furlongs, Woolwich, 1930s.

his brother Dick, it came to sell furniture by other designers. By the mid-1930s it had outgrown the premises and moved along the road, having the new showroom designed by Geoffrey Jellicoe. This caused something of a stir with its large plate glass frontage illuminated at night by blue neon tubes with a showroom some 120 ft long displaying Dick's furniture and his wife Marian Pepler's rugs, along with startling 'continental' furniture. Nikolaus Pevsner worked, for a time, as the Gordon Russell Ltd's buyer, and encouraged the firm to look to the continent. These premises, as those of Parker-Knoll, shut down during the war. When Gordon Russell's decided to reopen in London after the war, perhaps based on its expanding contract work, it was to be in very different surroundings – a grand Adam-ceilinged building in Stratford Place. It was, perhaps,

considered necessary to present a more solid image than that of plate glassed Wigmore Street, given the large sums involved in contract work.

A house in Knightsbridge served as the London showrooms for Betty Joel Ltd. to show off her Hollywood style modernist furniture in the early inter-war years. She displayed her furniture in some dozen rooms, which were frequented not so much by the design conscious visitors of Gordon Russell's, but by royalty and celebrities, the Mountbattens included. Betty's husband David, who was later to run the firm, described the building –

> …we had a shop window put in, always carefully dressed and lighted at night to take advantage of the magnificent site of our premises.

After the war Hille, yet another East End manufacturer who had moved out, first to Leytonstone and then to Watford, decided it needed to 'show off' in London. It had found introducing 'contemporary' furniture to 'reactionary' customers, as Rosamind Julius, the founder's grand-daughter described it, something of a struggle and took premises, in 1953, in Albemarle Street, off Piccadilly to see if this might improve sales; in 1962 these premises were redesigned by Peter Moro, with Robin Day responsible for the interiors. It was to become the mecca for cognoscenti, probably one of the most internationally recognized furniture showrooms in Europe. And the reputation of Hille was furthered by yet another building, that of its new Watford office, designed by Erno Goldfinger in 1961, its 'brutalist' style bringing much publicity and resultant visitors.

A rather looser example of clustering, of long standing in the furniture trade, was not along the streets of London, but around the chalky Chiltern hills centred on High Wycombe. Beech grows well on chalk and beech makes sturdy chairs. The early 'bodgers', whittling chair legs in the woods, began to be organized into workshops, which, in time, grew into factories. By the turn of the century Parkers (to become Parker-Knoll), late of Curtain

Opposite page left: Gordon Russell showroom, Wigmore Street, 1935. **Opposite page right:** Hille showroom, 1963. **Right:** Finmar London showroom, 1960s.

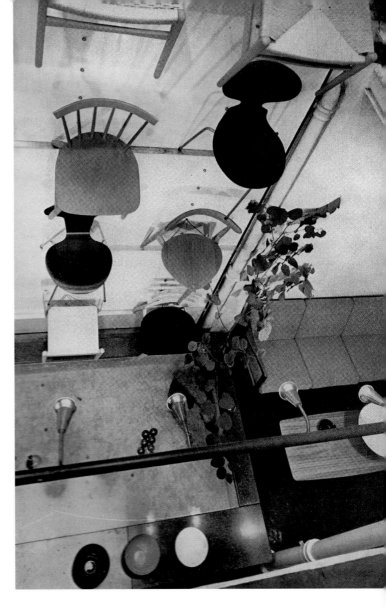

Road, decided to move to the area, to be joined by Ebenezer Gomme (later to produce G-Plan) and by Luciano Ercolani. Ercolani, who had actually worked with Gomme, established Furniture Industries Ltd. (Ercol) in the area in 1920, his factory eventually to cover a twelve acre site. As late as the 1950s it was estimated that there were some seven thousand people employed in the High Wycombe furniture industry. These did not present clustered façades that visitors could move along, as in London, spread as they were, but nevertheless, High Wycome furniture manufacturers would sometimes show together in exhibitions, presenting themselves as a High Wycombe section, hyping what was considered the attribute of their furniture – solid tradition.

In fact, out-of-town factory sites, in themselves, sometimes could be said to have made a contribution to furniture sales, in a small but significant way. Workshops morphed into factories when, with the coming of mechanization and mass production, furniture firms sought cheaper land for their expansion. Proprietors took a good deal of pride in these new works and would show off about

AERIAL · VIEW · OF
Hamptons Factories & Depositories
QUEEN'S ROAD, BATTERSEA, S.W.8

Opposite page: Hamptons factories and depositories, Battersea. **Above left:** Betty Joel factory, Kingston by-pass. **Above right:** Gordon Russell factory, opened 1935, Park Royal, west London.

them in their catalogues. It would be hoped that the size of the new sites, as well as the impressiveness of the buildings and machinery would be associated, in the public's mind, with the impressiveness of the products emerging. In this, Ercol's twelve acres and Lusty's seventeen acres were to be easily outdone by Harris Lebus, with its twenty eight acre site at Tottenham.

Hampton's, extolling its new Model Factories in 1926, provides an example of how 'the works' were frequently featured in furniture catalogues –

> ...has been thought out and planned expressly with a view to making them supreme Model Workshops in which shall be exemplified

conditions which are ideal, alike for workers and for the attainment of perfect finish in all the various goods manufactured.

Other companies went further, inviting potential customers to see 'the works' for themselves. Maples advertised its 'extensive upholstery and chair-making factories, cabinet works and bedding factories' which, being near the main shop, customers could visit to inspect the advanced machinery working. David Joel wrote quite blatantly of Betty Joel's efforts to lure people out to its factory on the Kingston by-pass –

> Here in the delightful atmosphere of scented tropical woods and of the charm and integrity

which real craftsmen possess, the customer was usually secured as a patron for all time.

And visitors would trudge out to Temple End, if not to see the Parker-Knoll factory, at least to visit its exceptional collection of antique furniture, built up over the years, and lodged there.

Of course the bulk of the country's furniture buyers were served either by floors in department stores in the nearest large centre, or, more probably, by the chains of furniture stores which mushroomed in the inter-war years. Some were regional as Jackson stores in Lancashire and Yorkshire, and Perrings, largely in the south, but others were more widely spread as Jays, The Times Furnishing Co.and Smart Bros. By 1939 it was estimated that some twenty nine firms had some six hundred branches. It was the Great Universal Stores (GUS), although primarily a general mail order company, which began acquiring furniture chains, such as Jays, Smarts and the British and Colonial Furniture Co., and which, by the late 50s, owned more than one thousand retail outlets, dominating the market. Although these shops might be distinguished from each other, as with the fascia typography of the Times Furnishing Co., they could not be said to have been architecturally distinguished, as would later be the Habitat stores.

Nevertheless 'modernism' for furniture, and for the buildings in which it was sold, seeped gradually into the larger towns and their suburbs, out of London. However, when the newly established evangelical Council of Industrial Design, in the post-war years, planned to put on a special series of local exhibitions of 'good taste', they seem to have found themselves obliged to work with local general department stores rather than furniture shops. An exception was Wylie & Lochhead's, then a major furniture firm in Glasgow, whose early Victorian building ('the most handsome erection for business purposes in Glasgow'), had been burnt down in 1883, only to be replaced by an even more impressive building of four galleried stories surrounding an atrium.

There were also some courageous stalwart independents fighting the good fight for 'good design' beyond London that need recognition.

Above: Aerial view of Lusty's Lloyd Loom factory site.

TUPPENCE PLAIN - PENNY COLOURED

When the Good Furniture Group of independent operators was founded in 1953, spurred on by Geoffrey Dunn of Dunn's of Bromley, it consisted of a select octet, including P.E. Gane of Bristol, Hening Bros. of Nottingham and Lee Longland & Co. of Derby.

Gane's had made something of a name for itself, when, for a brief period in the 1930s, it became associated with Marcel Breuer, one of the most significant talents to emerge from the Bauhaus. Breuer not only designed furniture for Gane's but, in 1936, designed its pavilion for the Royal Show, which by its avant garde design was made much of in the press.

Lee Longland had been established in 1902 and had early on impressed by its progressiveness with its

out-of-hours window display lighting in 1907 and its motorized delivery vans of 1912. Lee Longland can well be included as a firm that could attract customers by its architecture, with its new art deco building in 1932, in brick and Portland stone, and claiming, at the time, to be the only store out of London to have curved glass windows. It was still making news at the end of the period of this book with its, rare for the furniture trade, early television and radio advertising, its jingle 'Leave it, Leave it to Lee, Leave it to Lee Longland!'

As a small after thought on the link of buildings to furniture selling, it is worth noting that fires were not infrequent in furniture stores, as with Wylie and Lochhead, and although being seen no doubt as disaster in the immediate aftermath, would often be taken as opportunity to rebuild in styles more contemporary to the furniture being sold. When the old Dunn's store in the centre of Bromley was aflame in a 1941 bombing raid, it is reported that Geoffrey Dunn said 'Let it burn' – a modernist he wanted a modernist building and he got one.

Opposite page top: Original Dunn's of Bromley premises. **Opposite page bottom:** Rebuilt premises completed in 1949 following a bombing raid in 1941. Designed by architect Bertram Carter. **Left:** Alternate view of rebuilt premises.

And then, from time to time, often in specially designed buildings, furniture would be 'shown off' in exhibitions. In a paper for Manchester University, David Jeremiah wrote of the potential influence of these –

> Exhibitions on national and regional scales have provided defining moments in consumer values and those displays arranged through the collaboration of retail trade and professional organisations have been essential conduits of new ideas, conspiring to raise public expectations.

Jeremiah may, perhaps, have been a shade optimistic in stating the influence of exhibitions, particularly when one considers the furniture market, but there certainly were a considerable number of exhibitions in the fifty years of this book, governmental, professional and commercial, in which furniture was displayed. To what extent this affected furniture sales or public taste is yet to be proven, but at the very least, exhibitions gave manufacturers opportunity to show their wares and to publicise what they were about.

Opposite page: Arding & Hobbs stand, Ideal Home Exhibition, 1932. **Top and above:** Postcards of Oetzmann's cottages – furnished for 45gns. Japan British Exhibition, 1910.

Harrods

extend to all Interested in the Development of Up-to-date, Artistic and Labour-minimising Homes an Invitation to a Remarkable Exhibit revealing the wonderful possibilities in this direction opened up by Modern Home-Building Science

'MODERN HOMES'

The Exhibition is extremely comprehensive, showing every detail of the Modern Home worked out and clearly demonstrating how much can be done in making a Home Convenient and Beautiful without necessitating excessive outlay. No Modern Housewife should fail to see this Exhibition

HARRODS GREAT NEW EXHIBITION

THE Exhibition, while serving the general purpose outlined above, is also intended to show in particular the scope and possibilities of the various Inexpensive Furnishing Schemes which Harrods undertake. It is safe to say that many visitors will be absolutely astounded at the effect that can be achieved at no more than quite nominal cost. The Homes shown are in every sense of the word Modern,

The Palm Lounge, Harrods 'Modern Homes' Exhibition

Woodman Burbidge Managing Director

contributing equally to rest of body and ease of mind, catering as much for the æsthetic as for the practical sense. The Exhibition centres round a spacious Palm Lounge, where visitors may meet their friends or sit in comfort and take their notes. *To those who find it impracticable to come to Harrods, a copy of Harrods superbly-produced book 'Modern Homes' will be sent free on request.*

HARRODS LTD　　　　　　　　　**LONDON SW1**

Left: Advertisement from *The Sketch* for an exhibition at Harrods, 1922. **Opposite page:** Exhibition at Bowman Bros., 1951. **Opposite page top right and bottom:** Contemporary Exhibition, Harrison Gibson, Ilford, 1951.

Perhaps not what Jeremiah would include in his definition of exhibitions were the numerous ones advertised by retail furniture shops and stores, which, although hyped as exhibitions, were not much more than a special arrangement of a new stock range that had just arrived. But occasionally shop-based 'exhibitions' would be rather more than that as when, in 1949, David Morgan Ltd. of Cardiff set up five furnished rooms and a number of smaller laid out bays, with the title 'Background for Living' which ran for some six months.

One of the most significant inter-war store-based exhibitions was that held by Waring & Gillows in their Oxford Street emporium in 1928. It is said that Waring were nudged into action (as it had done little in the way of modernism up to that time), by a Shoolbred exhibition of the furniture designed by the French association DIM (Rene Joubert, George Mouveau and Philippe Petit), which had drawn good press notices.

Waring & Gillow trumpeted its exhibition –

The Exhibition is conceived on a scale that is altogether exceptional and represents the most liberally planned display of Modern Art in home decoration and furniture yet attempted in Europe or America.

and further –

Lord Waring's belief in the new movement should have important reactions on the furniture industries in the future.

The exhibition was designed by Paul Follot and Serge Chermayeff, the latter having been made Head of the Modern Art Studio at Waring & Gillow in 1928, and the exhibition including several of his pieces. Chermayeff left the company in 1931 to set up his own practice and, in fact, mounted furniture exhibitions in other stores, as Whiteley's. There is little evidence of the Waring & Gillow exhibition having the widespread effect that Lord Waring had predicted, although it was well received by the architectural fraternity and by design organisations as the Design

Right: Shoolbred exhibition poster, 1928, des. Paul E. Derrick advertising agency.
Far right: Brochure for Chermayeff exhibition at Waring & Gillow, 1928.

& Industries Association, and it certainly turned Waring & Gillow from its 'historic' tradition.

The store holding the most in-house furniture 'exhibitions', in the inter-war years, was Heal's. Throughout the period it advertised special displays as 'exhibitions', as well as those it mounted in its Mansard Gallery. Early ones were entitled 'Modern Tendencies', and, with the depression and its after years 'Better Furniture for Better Times',

'Heal's Economy Furniture' and 'Economy with a Difference'. Post-war it put on annual exhibitions of new designs, which included furniture by Christopher Heal. Two such shows which impressed the press, were 'Design for the Future', to celebrate Heal's one hundred and fiftieth anniversary, for which it manufactured designs invited from seven countries; and a rather odd one, in 1968, 'Living with Children', for which Heal's had chairs suspended from an overhead railway.

Left: Chermayeff exhibition at Whiteley's, 1934. Right: Poster for Heal's furniture exhibition, des. Norman Weaver.

Susanna Gooden, in her history of Heal's, wrote of its exhibitions that they –

> ...were extremely varied and managed to work on many levels being inspiring to designers and education, and to the general public, without being condescending, fashionable but approachable, revolutionary but with inevitable commercial undertones.

Actual furniture trade shows, on exhibition sites, had been held from the turn of the century, as an annual Furniture Trade Exhibition and Market being recorded in 1896 at Olympia, and further ones at the Agricultural Halls in Islington. Subsequent ones seem to have received little notice in the general press being largely eclipsed by the government sponsored British Industries Fairs, which ran annually from 1915 to 1954, and the Daily Mail Ideal Home Exhibitions, which were to

Above: Misha Black designed furniture exhibition, Earls Court, 1958. **Opposite page:** Princess Margaret visiting 'Beautility' furniture exhibit, Earls Court, 1950s. **Opposite page top right:** Dunn's of Bromley stand at the British Industries Fair, 1947. **Opposite page bottom right:** H. Morris & Co. stand at the British Industries Fair, 1949.

run for over a hundred years, from 1908 to 2009, both altogether with higher profiles, better financed and better designed. *Art & Industry* wrote of the Furniture Exhibition –

> The British Furniture Exhibition was in danger of becoming something of a music hall joke in design circles. Both the show itself, as a piece of exhibition design, and the exhibits, were the butts of facetious comment of one sort or another by those who were in a position to make the inevitably odious comparisons between the reality of the exhibition as it stood, and the standards achieved elsewhere, notably on the continent.

Things began to improve when the Council of Industrial Design took a space in the show in 1957 and when Misha Black was commissioned to design the public section. His 'xylon' curtain of wooden leaves, 60 feet wide and 100 feet high, brought the Furniture Exhibition into the public eye. Towards the end of our period, in 1968, a display that again made the press, was when Gomme introduced G-Plan in the High Wycombe section of the

1 Main Entrance Beautility Stand Furniture Exhibition.
2. Corner of the interior.
3. H.R.H. Princess Margaret being greeted when visiting the stand.

Exhibition. There was something of a stir with the display, thought up by J. Walter Thompson, of a white leather cloth floor inlaid with marble and curtains of leopard skin to show off the new range.

Furniture displayed at the Ideal Home Exhibitions in the early 1920s has been described as 'still determinedly tudor, with historic trade pieces alongside arts and crafts ones'. Ambrose Heal was altogether more optimistic about these exhibitions encouraging modern furniture design in his description of the 1929 Ideal Home Exhibition –

> At many of the larger stands representing the general furnishing trade, hardly an antique or reproduction was to be seen...I noticed how the crowd was decidedly drawn to the modern.

Heal's was to mount its own curiosity for the 1931 Ideal Home Exhibition, thought up by Prudence

Maufe and based on the tale of the princess and the pea. It consisted of an enormous canopied bed piled high with mattresses, the attention it received said to have miffed Oetzmann's, whose traditional stand was alongside.

Misha Black probably summed up reasonably well the furniture displays at the Ideal Home Exhibition, both pre-war and post-war –

> ...the solid background of the British furnishing trade being often spiced with the thinly distributed pepper of contemporary design of a very high standard...

Certainly, still, into the 1960s, the firms showing were a mixture of old-established and new boys, the Times Furnishing Company and Waring & Gillow

'spiced', as Black put it, by Minty, and Nathan. When the Ideal Home did attempt something beyond this acceptable balance of traditional and contemporary, as when, in 1956, Alison and Peter Smithson were let loose for 'The House of the Future', the result was considered so eccentric as to be incomprehensible to most of the visitors. The Daily Mail understood its market and generally kept focused on it. Although other newspapers, as the Daily Herald in the 1940s and the Sunday Times at Harrods in 1964, tried their hands at furniture exhibitions, none were ever in serious competition.

Meanwhile furniture was being exhibited on a much more sophisticated stage – the international exhibition. In the fifty years of this book there were literally dozens of international exhibitions mounted across the world, major and minor,

governmental and trade. The British government seems generally to have been luke-warm about most of these, and where they did contribute, the effort was frequently half-hearted with a tight budget, and furniture does not appear to have featured large. There is a record of the British Institute of Industrial Art inviting Gabe & Pass to show in the 1925 Paris Industrial Exhibition, but as the firm, in 1947, was still showing bergere suites, one cannot imagine its contribution remarkable.

Although there are odd examples of British furniture being shown abroad, as when Gordon Russell showed in the 1930 Moza Exhibition of Industrial and Decorative Art, it was not until the Paris Exhibition of 1937 that the British government threw its weight, and budget, into an international exhibition, when it appointed Frank Pick and Oliver

Hill to be responsible for the British Pavilion. But although Heal's with Christopher Heal was brought in to design some of the rooms, and Gordon Russell furniture was also on display, the theme chosen – 'British Life' – was generally panned for the reason Misha Black gave – 'albeit the way of life that only 5% of the population can afford'.

Even post-war, at the Brussels World Fair in 1958, the British contribution was drowned in Commonwealth flags, historical roses, pubs and hunting, and more of the ilk. And at Montreal's Expo 67, although it was determined that this time the British display should be 'contemporary' – Carnaby Street etc – it was still full of whimsy, supplied by James Gardner.

When it came to flying the flag for furniture one of

the biggest showings was for a little remembered exhibition, the Central African Rhodes Centenary Exhibition in Bulawayo in 1953, where although the 'old boys' – Heal's and Gordon Russell – were still central, they were joined by newer players – Geoffrey Dunn, Ernest Race, Hille, Pel, Primavera, and, from Scotland, the Scottish Furniture Manufacturers and the Scottish Cooperative Wholesale Society.

When Hille and Race decided to show at the Tenth Triennale in Milan in 1954, *Art & Industry* wrote blatantly –

While the Governments of Austria, Canada, France, Italy, Spain, Belgium, Holland, Germany, Switzerland, Israel and the Scandinavian countries participated ... the British Government declined an invitation to take part.

Showing off furniture overseas was largely left to individual enterprise as when Hille and Robin Day showed at the Milan Triennale, Day winning a gold medal for his BA3 chair, and Ernest Race showed off his designs on a stand designed by Misha Black, of the Design Research Unit, which must have been a considerable investment for his firm. Day and

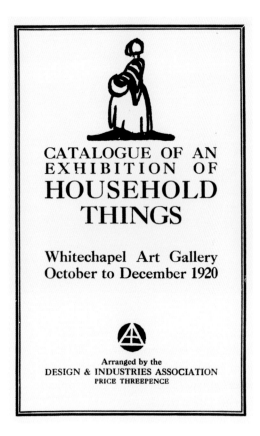

CATALOGUE OF AN
EXHIBITION OF
**HOUSEHOLD
THINGS**

Whitechapel Art Gallery
October to December 1920

Arranged by the
DESIGN & INDUSTRIES ASSOCIATION
PRICE THREEPENCE

Above: DIA exhibition catalogue, Whitechapel Art Gallery, 1920. **Opposite page left:** DIA 'Register your choice' exhibit, Charing Cross Station, 1953. **Opposite page right:** Betty Joel at 'British Art in Industry' exhibition, Royal Academy, 1935.

his assistant Clive Latimer had previously entered a competition for the design of low cost furniture, run by MOMA in New York in 1948, for which they won first prize; MOMA was to take their entry into its permanent collection. Race was later to show abroad again, as when he showed his Cormorant chair at the California State Exhibition of 1961, also winning a gold medal.

Interwoven with these exhibitions, in the inter- and early post-war years, neither patriotic nor blatantly commercial, were those evangelically bent on education, on raising standards, both of production and of aesthetics, mounted to influence manufacturers, retailers, designers and the general public alike. In the inter-war years, these were laid on by the Design & Industries Association, with some essays into the field by the Royal Society of Arts and by the government Institute of Industrial Art; in the post-war years it was the Council of Industrial Design that led the way. The Design & Industries Association (DIA) had its roots in arts and crafts and it is not without significance that until the war its headquarters was at the Art Workers Guild. However, its aim was to ensure

that 'machine work may be more beautiful by appropriate handling', and to encourage 'a more intelligent demand amongst the public for what is best and soundest in design'.

When it came to mounting exhibitions DIA was most active in the 1920s starting with its 'Exhibition of Household Things' in 1920, held at the Whitechapel Art Gallery. This included furniture from Heal's, Harrods, Arding & Hobbs, Drage and Oetzmann. In 1921 it held similar exhibitions at the South London Art Gallery and the Manchester City Art Gallery. DIA also contributed to the Ideal Home Exhibitions and developed display schemes for retailers to use, the initial one going to Bowmans. Although DIA's use of exhibitions to educate waned,

it did mount an exhibition after the war, in 1953, at Charing Cross station, entitled 'Register Your Choice', for which visitors were asked to vote as which of the two rooms displayed they preferred – one chosen by DIA, one by the National Association of Retail Furnishers. It was visited by some 30,000 people, who voted, luckily for DIA, in the ratio three to two in its favour.

An exhibition mounted in response to the governmental concern about design standards, that had been contained in the Gorrell Report on Art & Industry, was one held at the Dorland Hall in 1933 – 'British Industrial Art in Relation to the Home'. This was arranged by Oliver Hill and contained a number of rooms which are worth recording for their mix of

designers, Heal and Russell being to the fore –

Dining room	Ambrose Heal
Bedroom	Raymond McGrath
Living room	R.W. Symonds
Study	R.D. Russell
Minimum flat	Wells Coates
Bathroom	Oliver Hill
Weekend house	Serge Chermayeff
Dining room	Oliver Hill
Aga kitchen	Mrs. Darcy Braddell
Gas kitchen	Wells Coates

As with so many of these well-meaning exhibitions, aimed at educating the masses, it tended to show what was actually only accessible to the few.

Athough there had been a 'good taste' exhibition at the Victoria & Albert Museum at the time of the British Empire Exhibition, which appears to have been organized by Ambrose Heal and Gordon Russell working in cohoots, the one that made most of a stir in the inter-war years was the 1935 'British Art in Industry' at the Royal Academy. Mounted by an executive committee drawn from the Royal Society of Arts (RSA) and the Royal Academy, it had an advisory committee for each type of product to be shown. It was said to be the first public industrial exhibition in England where no payment was required from exhibitors, who were selected by the sectional committees, as Gordon Russell wrote 'without fear or favour'. The furniture section included Gordon Russell, Heal's, Waring

& Gillow, Harrods, the Bath Cabinet Makers and William Whiteley's. Striving to show off pieces not generally to be seen elsewhere, it included such luxurious designs as those for Betty Joel's art deco bedroom. The exhibition was consequently panned in the press as showing goods that only the affluent could afford, and as showing how out of touch the organisers were with the needs, tastes and purses of the public. As an aside, the exhibition did make the not inconsiderable breakthrough, however, of displaying the designers' names by their products, a rarity until then. The RSA made a further attempt to get its message across in 1948 with its exhibition of the work of its Royal Designers for Industry (RDI), again mounted at the Royal Academy. This was supported by the new Council of Industrial Design and had Gordon Russell chairing its executive committee.

By the end of WWII the Council of Industrial Design (CoID) had been established and was eager to flex its evangelical muscles. As early as 1946 it was mounting an ambitious exhibition at the Victoria & Albert Museum, which has been extremely well documented – 'Britain Can Make It' (BCMI). Stafford Cripps of the Board of Trade was eager that the exhibition should include prototypes in order to stimulate industry converting, as it was at the time, from munitions to peace time production. Consequently much of the furniture on show was, as James Gardner remarked, more in the nature of concepts of what might be than

Professor R.D. Russell designs for Harris
Lebus, 'Design at Work' exhibition, 1948.

what was actually available. The rooms on show
were designed for fictitious families and included
pieces from Ercol, Heal's and Race. If an exhibition's
success is to be judged by numbers, then BCMI
certainly was one, with nearly a million and a half
visitors. But it left much frustration in that little
of what was on show could be found in the shops.
Nevertheless the exhibition gave some designers
good exposure; there is a report that both Dunn's
and Heal's on seeing Race designs immediately put
orders in, whilst the government purchased over a
thousand Race pieces to furnish troop ships. *Picture
Post*, representing the common man, wrote of
'Britain Can Make It' –

> ...in the welter of stripes and spots and
> whitewood and home-spun it would have been
> almost a relief to see a vast chintz armchair.

Milner Gray, from a designer's point of view
recorded that it seemed like –

> ...a large shop where you had to pay for the
> privilege of getting in, knowing in advance that
> you wouldn't be allowed to buy the goods when

Leaflet announcing the opening of the Design Centre, 1953.

you got there…(yet they stood) hour after hour on the Kensington pavement.

A Mass Observation survey at the time came up with the figure of 80% of visitors really enjoying the exhibition, but the majority feeling that their tastes had not been changed by it.

Penny Sparke in *Did Britain Make It?* has it that the CoID saw most furniture retailers as 'evil manipulators of working class taste' and certainly, through the 50s and 60s it went about its work in a crusading manner – organizing travelling exhibitions shown in art galleries and other public venues, designing exhibition layouts for shops and stores, and showing exhibitions in key provincial stores as Wylie & Lochhead in Glasgow, Garlands in Norwich, Schofields in Leeds, Grants in Croydon and Affleck & Brown in Manchester.

But perhaps CoID exerted most influence on furniture buyers' taste when it set up its own permanent exhibition space in the Design Centre in the Haymarket. This was sometimes referred to as 'a showroom for the nation', open to all, and, indeed,

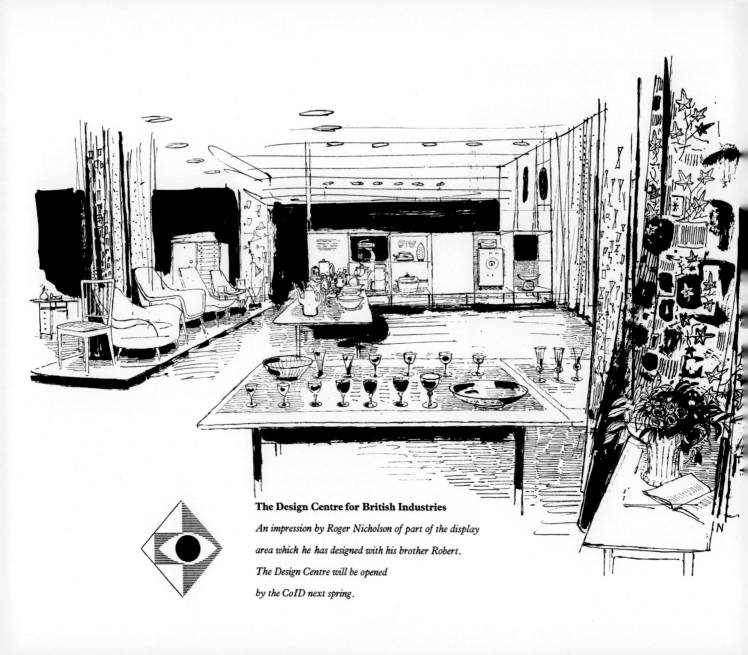

The Design Centre for British Industries

An impression by Roger Nicholson of part of the display

area which he has designed with his brother Robert.

The Design Centre will be opened

by the CoID next spring.

by the late 1960s it was receiving some 3,000 visitors each day. Its Design Centre Awards (dominated in the early years by Hille and Race) and its Design Centre Label, launched to assure potential buyers that it approved the article, furthered the cause of good taste and good standards. David Joel wrote optimistically of the effect of the Council's Design Centre –

> This Centre has had an immense influence on the public, on the press, on retail buyers and on foreign visitors to London.

A curious hybrid exhibition to raise tastes was held in 1952, combining the social work concerns of Oxford House in Bethnal Green with the aesthetic education concerns of the Whitechapel Art Gallery. Titled 'Setting Up Home' and designed by Anthony Lewis it showed room settings to encourage young couples setting up home to buy well.

The Festival of Britain does not fall neatly into any of the previous categories of exhibition for it did not set out to push good design and certainly not to sell anything. Yet by including contemporary furniture not only in some of its displays but in its public areas, it actually provided young designers with a platform, as the youthful Terence Conran having some of his work showing in the Princess Flying Boat in the Transport Pavilion; Dunn's and the Furniture Industries Ltd. were featured in the Power and Production section of the Festival of

1951 year of Achievement

The 1951 Festival of Britain will highlight the wonderful achievements and aspirations of British craftsmanship... and in the world of furnishing, 1951 will be a year when Nathan Dining Room furniture will again stand in the forefront for specialised production and advanced design.

NATHAN

The accepted name for Better Quality Furniture

B. & I. NATHAN LIMITED, ANGEL ROAD, EDMONTON, LONDON, N.18   TOT 2246/7

Britain. But the bulk of the furniture featured in displays were, obviously, in the Homes and Gardens section, eccentrically showing a series of rooms, as those for an elderly lady, a headmaster, a business man, and more of the same. Now familiar names as Heal's, Hille, Stag, Race, Gomme, Story, Wylie & Lochhead, Morris of Glasgow and Gordon Russell were some that were included, along with less familiar names as Ginson & Slater of Nottingham, Fothergill & Harvey of Manchester and R.W. Toothill of Durham. Although, presumably, the selectors had tried to have as wide a sample of the furniture industry as they could, it was estimated that less than 10% was represented.

Although, in retrospect, the Festival has received much criticism as displaying more of what had been achieved than courageously pointing to the future, it certainly did influence the taste of the general public, who were, as it were, catching up, giving them the opportunity to see much good design that they would not have had the opportunity to see otherwise. Hazel Conway, in her book on Ernest Race, states firmly that the Festival had been the salvation of his company, his Antelope and

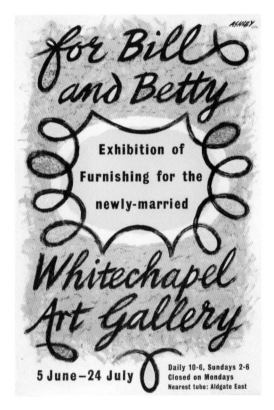

Ashley Havinden poster for Whitechapel Art Gallery, 'for Bill and Betty', 1952.

Springbok chairs being used for both indoor and outdoor public places.

David Jeremiah went even further, in his groundbreaking book *Architecture and Design for the Family in Britain* –

> It was the Festival of Britain that provided the CoID with the opportunity to secure the refined Contemporary style that it had adopted as its own as the taste of the nation, and also created a climate that stimulated interest in popular taste, design progress and the British tradition of the well-made craft object.

In finely figured M
Comprising :
4 ft. 0 ins. wide,
large hanging
ment. 3 ft. 6 ins.
Table. 2 ft. 6 ins.
Cabinet, 4 ft. 0
fitted with 4 shelv
at our Lancaster

£59 · 18

Stool to match £

Or 36 Monthly Pa
£1 . 15 .

'NORWOOD' BEDSTEAD. An attractive bedstead
beautifully made with Mahogany. Fitted with steel
sides and end rails. (B. 432).
3 ft. size £9 . 15 . 0   4 ft. 6 ins. size £12 . 12 . 0

THE 'KINGSTON' SUITE

finely figured Walnut.
he Wardrobe 4 ft. 0 ins.
ide, fitted for hanging
othes and provided with

From the mid-19th century onwards the catalogue has been a crucial medium for the selling of furniture, not only because it reached those who were unable to travel to a shop or store, but because most retail outlets could only carry a relatively small amount of any manufacturer's range of goods at any one time. Even those manufacturers who had their own showrooms could rarely put on display all the colour, pattern, and design combinations and permutations they were able to produce.

In an issue in 1952 of the magazine *Design*, put out by the Council of Industrial Design, an idea was put forward that there was a strong correlation between the design of a catalogue and the character of the furniture illustrated in it – that 'well-designed' furniture would be featured in an equally well-designed catalogue – in its layout, typography and illustration; much the same argument as has been made here for furniture 'buildings'. The example given in the article was a catalogue produced for the Scottish Furniture Manufacturers –

The new Scottish furniture catalogue...seems brightly anxious both in colour (yellow, red and

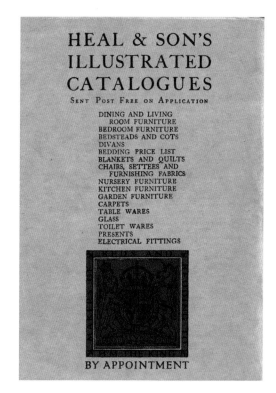

Opposite page: Excerpt from Warings catalogue. **Above:** List of Heal's sectional catalogues available on request, 1934.

Wolfe & Hollander catalogue in unusual landscape format, 1936.

black on pale green) and complexity to impress the reader that contemporary furniture is an art worthy of a portfolio; the folder is not easy to handle with its loose unbound sheets tucked in a red cover inside a folded envelope. This polished presentation well matches the original and costly furniture inside.

In fact furniture catalogues, over the years, have come in all shapes and sizes, with a variety of tricks to attract the would-be customer, sometimes in harmony with the design of the furniture being illustrated, sometimes not.

Maple and Heal's were two of the earliest firms to produce catalogues. Maple advertised the availability of its catalogue in the 1860s as 'a new illustrated catalogue containing prices of every article required for completely furnishing a house of any class, post free.' Heal's catalogue was, initially, not much more than a mail order price list, as an 1860 one entitled 'Bedsteads, Bedding and Bedroom Furniture for India, China and the Colonies'. Gradually the Heal's lists morphed into what now would be recognized as a catalogue, and more than that, as a 'production'. When Ambrose Heal's designs first appeared in an 1898 catalogue, the

Maples 'Modern Furniture for Modern Homes' catalogue cover with cut-out window, undated.

Unconventional furniture catalogue for Maple & Co. with faux stained-glass cover, undated.

Example of faux material on front of
Bowmans catalogue, undated.

Example of imitation wood on front of Morris
& Co. of Glasgow catalogue, 1940s.

TUPPENCE PLAIN - PENNY COLOURED

Builder's Journal made special note of it –

> It is rarely indeed that we receive a trade
> catalogue which is so pleasant to handle, to look
> upon, and to read...

The permutations and combinations offered in
furniture catalogues when it comes to dimensions
and construction have been countless. Produced
either portrait or landscape, the inter-war
catalogues were frequently hundreds of pages,
Drage's, possibly, making the record with one
covering some three hundred and six pages. But
the impressiveness of size could well depend on the
quality and thickness of the paper used. One put out
by Gordon Russell in the 1930s, which, although
only having 36 pages, had chosen to use expensive
thick paper, which, along with a pocket attached
to the back page and a suede-like cover, gave it a
greater impact than the hundred or more pages of
the catalogues of the like of the Hackney Furnishing
Company, Wolfe & Hollander and Waring. So big
did catalogues become that many had to resort
to indexes. Dividing up the contents was usually
achieved by a conventional contents page or index

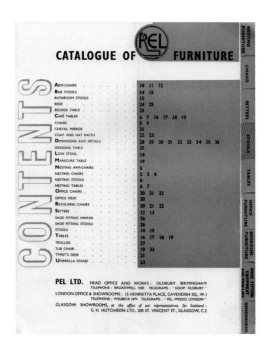

Left: Pel furniture catalogue. An example of indented index tabs to ease viewing. **Above:** Example of post-war indexing, Austinsuite. **Opposite page:** Contents page of early Harris Lebus catalogue.

list, but there were innovative variations, as that of Wolfe & Hollander which had a broad white margin to the right of each page with sideways printing of the various sections, or that of Pel which actually had the pages indented with a different coloured edging for each section.

These mammoth productions were financially costly. At one time Bowmans actually had printed on their catalogues 'If you don't need this expensively produced book please do not throw it away. Pass it on to a friend who may be interested and accept the grateful thanks of Bowman.' As it was found that many potential buyers were only interested in a certain range of items, a number of furniture companies dealt with the problem of size by having, in addition to the comprehensive catalogue, a series of smaller ones. Maples, at one time, had some nineteen sectional catalogues, which they would send out on request. Heal's had sixteen of what they termed 'specials', as, for example, 'nursery furniture' and 'reasonable furniture'.

INDEX

Catalogue cover for 'The Great Universal Stores: London, Manchester, Glasgow'.

Illustrated cover for Drages Christmas catalogue, with stories by well-known authors.

Lloyd Loom

Registered Trade Mark

Woven Fibre Furniture

BRITISH MADE

Telegrams:
"Comparison, Bochurch,"
London

HEAD OFFICE and WORKS:

BROMLEY - BY - BOW
LONDON, E. 3
Telephone: EAST 5020 (6 lines)

London Showrooms:
79-81 PAUL STREET
FINSBURY, LONDON, E.C. 2
Telephone: CLERKENWELL 4541

Sole Manufacturers:

W. LUSTY & SONS LTD

ESTABLISHED
1872

Catalogue for Lloyd Loom, Woven Fibre Furniture, W. Lusty & Sons Ltd.

Landscape format catalogue for Jas. Shoolbred & Co. Ltd.

The Times Furnishing Company's

PLANNED HOMES

PLANNING A LOUNGE

Example of Times Furniture Co. sectional catalogue.

Oetzmann furniture catalogue, 1949.

The Times Furnishing Company brought out a more obviously advisory series – 'The Planned Home' – which consisted of smaller pamphlets to supplement its catalogue – 'Planning a Lounge', 'Planning a two room Flat', 'Planning a Sitting Room with a south facing window'!

The criticized Scottish Furniture Manufacturers's catalogue was not the only one to experiment with folders and the like. The Times Furnishing Company had previously had an envelope containing a series of separate leaflets on different aspects of furnishing; whilst post-war both Primavera and Race had folders, Race's with a large pull-out folded sheet illustrating its latest offerings. Race also tried out one held together by a rubber band which *Design* considered 'ingenious' as it allowed additional leaves to be easily inserted. Habitat's first catalogue, put out in 1966, came merely as line drawings on coloured paper fixed together at one corner – over-ambitious as it did not have the stock ready to meet the demand the 'catalogue' stirred up. Another eccentric offering was that of the Times Furnishing Company which tried out a catalogue in a magazine format, entitled *Good Furnishing*, which not only brought readers up to date with its latest furniture designs, but had articles on health and beauty, and even knitting

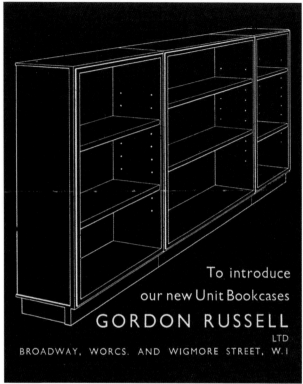

To introduce
our new Unit Bookcases
GORDON RUSSELL
LTD
BROADWAY, WORCS. AND WIGMORE STREET, W.1

Left: Catalogue cover for HK Furniture, undated.
Above: Spare design for booklet cover introducing
Gordon Russell's Unit Bookcases, undated.

Below: Utility Furniture brochure, undated.

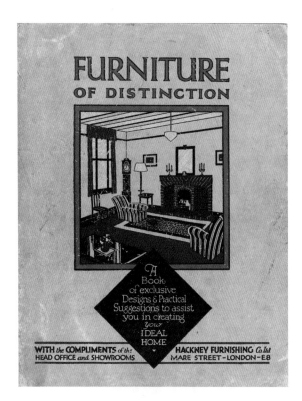

Above: Furniture catalogue for Hackney Furnishing Co. Ltd. of Mare Street, London, undated. **Opposite page:** Bowmans catalogue with pocket containing useful tape measure, *c.*1930s.

patterns! Drage had previously had a Christmas catalogue issue, containing short stories by well-known authors.

When it came to actual design, rather than structure, most of the inter-war furniture catalogues had simple covers, merely bearing the company's name. But others attempt to distinguish theirs by having specially textured covers, as Gordon Russell's and Waring's; whilst others had variations of cut-out windows exposing a view of a house or a room, as Maples's. A particularly ingenious and useful cover was one of Bowmans which had a small paper house attached to the front cover, in the form of a pocket containing a tape measure.

But generally it cannot be said that furniture catalogues made their mark in graphic design history in the fifty years covered by this book. Their purpose was to sell, and most often this meant cramming in as many illustrations of stock as was possible. Barely any mention, even in the smallest of print, was ever made of who had designed a catalogue; presumably, up to WWII, they were

THIS HOUSE IS FURNISHED WITH A 12 FOOT TAPE MEASURE DIVIDED INTO TWENTY INCH SECTIONS

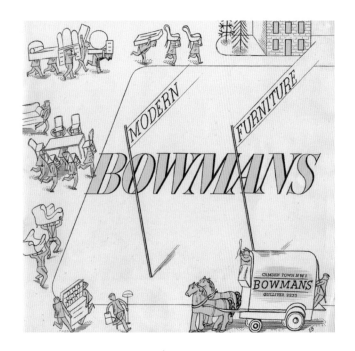

more often put together by the proprietor, or a senior manager of the firm, in cahoots with a local printer. Heal's, an exception, certainly made use of external artists for its catalogues from the turn of the century, as using Gregory Brown, a leading graphic designer in the 1920s, along with the likes of McKnight Kauffer and Herry Perry, both of whom were known through their work for London Transport. And no doubt Ambrose's hand was also on the catalogues as on most aspect of design at Heal's.

Another exception was Bowmans who, at one time or another, commissioned both Edward Bawden and Barnett Freedman. The Bawden illustration for a 1930s catalogue wittily showed delivery men rushing to get Bowmans furniture to people's homes. Freedman's was immediately recognizable by his iconic typography. Marcus Brumwell, the director of Stuart's advertising agency, which Bowmans used in the 1930s wrote in *Art & Industry* of how good it was to work with the firm to produce its catalogues. He described

Far left: Illustrated page from Bowmans catalogue, Edward Bawden, 1930s. Left and right: Two Barnett Freedman typographic catalogue covers for Bowmans, undated.

how Bowmans started the production relationship by explaining the firm's current policy in order to give the agency some flavour of the message it wanted to communicate. Bowmans would also select and nurture the photographer to be involved 'until he is head and shoulders above all furniture photographers in London', and work with the agency's copy writers to develop a story line to guide the photographic work. Bowmans made use of unoccupied rooms in its vast store to build up room settings with dummy windows and fireplaces, with

meticulous attention down to detail, such as cinders in the hearth, half-opened books, and spectacles lying on tables, to give the impression of lived-in rooms. Brumwell estimated it took the photography for a Bowmans catalogue up to three months to complete. Brumwell rounded off his article, which was on a catalogue designed by Freedman, with some smugness –

We think that most people will agree that the resulting catalogue is rather lovely – but with

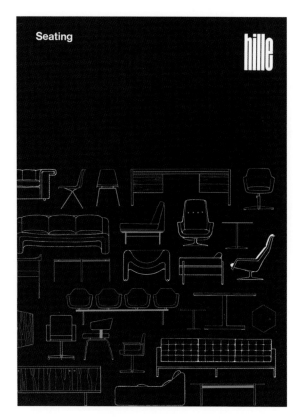

Above: Post-war catalogue cover for Hille.
Opposite page: Early loose-leaf catalogue for Habitat, 1960s.

such go-ahead people as Bowmans to work for, it should be good.

In the post-war period Robin Day is recorded to have been responsible for anything Hille did which involved design, so it is assumed this would have included catalogues; and certainly Conran was very much in charge when it came to the early Habitat ones, working along with Guy Fortescue. In contrast to Bowmans meticulous productions, the early Habitat catalogues were produced on the hoof in Conran's barn at his Suffolk cottage with his French photographer friend, Roger Gain, the shoot taking no more than three weeks. Habitat's later catalogues, however, as its empire expanded, were to involve large production teams of art directors, photographers and support staff. It was Conran, who was to break so many of the traditions of the furniture trade, who had his catalogues full of people actually using furniture – people were a rarity in furniture publicity, as will be noted again in the section on advertising. Conran's people clambered over his catalogues – children in bed, mums snuggled into armchairs, shoes cast off, dad putting together flat-pack furniture, and so on.

Habitat Desk

Desks do not have to be dull - a shiny white top with three black, white or orange drawers each side.
£29. 17. 6

Basket Chair and Sofa

Woven white willow for lazing away the days - in a sociable sofa or solitary chair.
Basket chair £5. 5. 0   sofa £11. 5. 0

Bertoia Chair

Bertoia chair with chrome web back, spikey legs and black cushion. Also available with back and legs white nylon coated.
chrome frame   £13. 18. 0
white frame   £8. 16. 6

3302 Sofa

Take two at a time of Conran's two-seater sofas.   Reasonably priced and unbelievably comfortable, they look great in all kinds of fabric.   Matching chairs and also three-seat sofas.
from £64. 19. 0

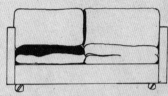

SU38 Daybed and SU39 Armchair

To spend a third of your life in,the Conran SU38 daybed is not enough - so sit smugly on it during the day as well.   Natural or scarlet beech frame with an interior sprung mattress and buttoned cushions in a wide selection of fabrics.Matching SU39 armchair.
SU38   from £59. 10. 0
SU39   from £28. 10. 0

T.1 Chair

Nuts and bolts tightly hold this chair together - and it stacks neatly away. Super waterproof coloured canvas and black or nylon dipped frame.From £16. 10. 0

Habitat Chesterfield

Lord Chesterfield would still be proud of his sofa whether upholstered in 19th century silk or a pop print.Comfortable and elegant with a sprung seat and plain or buttoned back and arms.   The legs can be stained to match the cover.
unbuttoned from £83. 10. 0 according to cover
buttoned   from £97. 10. 0 according to cover

6108 Single Pedestal Table

Conversation is easy round this white Conran dining table for two or four.   Heat resisting white melamine top and kick proof white pedestal.
£26. 5. 0

Bo-ex Chair

Bat wing chair with collapsible chrome frame.For the practical there is black, khaki,natural and orange canvas or for the hedonistic,black and brown hide or brown suede
from £11. 15. 0

habitat

77-79 Fulham Road London SW3   01-589 3277
Open Mon-Sat 9.30-6.00, late night Thursday to 8.00

156-158 Tottenham Court Road London W1
01-387 3242
Open Mon-Sat 9.30-6.00, late night Thursday to 8.00

14-16 Eden Walk Kingston upon Thames Surrey
01-549 0941
Open Mon-Sat 9.30-6.00, late night Friday to 7.30

14 John Dalton Street Manchester 2
061-832 8547
Open Mon-Sat 9.30-6.00, late night Thursday to 7.30

What must have been a first, and possibly unique, was a Conran cover, in 1969, giving an aerial view of a family sitting around a table having breakfast, the tops of their heads featuring large.

In the inter-war years most furniture catalogues illustrated their wares in black and white, whether by drawings, etchings, scraperboard, or, later on, photography, albeit occasionally an odd water colour might appear. This meant that textures and surfaces, such key characteristics of furniture, could not fully be appreciated by most of the offerings. Colour photography only really came into its own for the catalogues in the post-war years, albeit the more design conscious firms, as Race and Pel, produced some of their most striking covers in black and white at this time. But if impact was lacking for many of the visuals, so that it was frequently difficult to distinguish one suite of furniture from another, all seeming much of a

muchness, copy took over to assure the potential buyer of the qualities not easily discerned in the illustrations.

When it came to copy, most inter-war catalogues contained 'mission statements', communications from the proprietor, many written as personal notes and finished with the flourish of the great man's signature. Most tended to include wording to reassure the reader, as 'long tradition', 'craftsmanship' and the like. And many had the strut, the pomposity, the smugness, that were, possibly, actually attributes of the writer of the message. One of Drage's 'mission-statements' virtually linked the act of buying furniture, particularly the buying of their furniture, to the essence of living –

> The policy of the House of Drage summed up in one word is – VALUE
>
>> Value in furniture
>> Value in personal service
>> Value in home furnishing
>
> Home is the foundation of society, its

surroundings the greatest influence on life and character.

And the benevolence and charitable nature of Mr. Drage was extended even to those who did not buy –

> whether you place your order in my hands or elsewhere I wish you good luck, contentment, and happiness.

Heal's and Gordon Russell's messages of good design tended to have a 'holier than thou' tone, albeit with some occasional barbed comment on market rivals as Russell's –

> Freakish 'modernistic' designs soon pall, but you will find that our furniture carries on the great tradition of English cabinet making.

and as Heal's, in its 1934 'Reasonable Furniture' catalogue –

> In choosing the word 'Reasonable' as a title we have in mind something more than the mere

Exceptional black and white catalogue for
Race furniture, undated.

colloquial use of the word by which it is made
synonymous with 'cheap'.

Even the government in its 1943 Utility Furniture
catalogue had a degree of smugness –

All that you see with Utility Furniture is pure, it's
good – the more simple the furniture the more
precise must be the workmanship.

Pride extended, on occasions, beyond the actual
furniture, to the factories that produced the
furniture, and even to the transport that delivered
it, so that the excellence claimed for these would
somehow become associated with the furniture
itself.

Maples, in its lauding of its vehicles, was able
to assure its customers of the principled way it
operated generally, there being much outrage in the
1920s as to the possible pollution of the countryside
by advertising –

Our Green Delivery Vans are seen in almost
every county of England, threading through

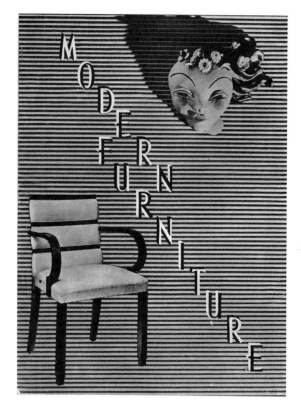

Times Furnishing Co. catalogue cover design.
A conventional firm attempting a modern cover.

towns, villages and country lanes alike, their appearance not violating the pastoral beauty of the English countryside.

(The green Maples vans clearly named with the Tottenham Court Road address were distinguished in carrying troops during WWI)

At least Bowmans, in extolling its fleet, was prepared to employ just a tinge of humour –

> We are specialists at the removal game. Our big modern vans all have pneumatic tyres to ensure a smooth passage for furniture and we have a well-trained band of stalwart men who do the work and who haven't been known to drop a catch yet.

Humour, as the reader may well have come to realize by now, was not a noticeable feature of furniture trading. A rare example was Parker-Knoll having a full page of copy introduction to one of its catalogues in the form of a meeting being opened –

Pel catalogue with effective use of black and white photography.

Chairman: *Ladies and Gentlemen ... be seated.*

Speaker: *I'm to tell you of the wonderful PK chair.*

Chairman: *Enough! Ladies and gentlemen let us adjourn to the following pages and let them speak for themselves.*

One of the most literary offerings was penned by the Buoyant Upholstery Company of Nottingham –

And in an age which is marked above all things by hurry and haste, in an age pre-eminently of locomotion, in which invention eats away time and space, it is something to have brought to perfection a restful thing, a thing which will tempt a man home and keep him there, in which he can listen to music and day-dream and practice the wise art of doing nothing at all.

Presumably the wife is busy putting the children to bed and cooking the supper, worrying, meanwhile, about what her husband might have been up to, out gallivanting, if they hadn't bought the Buoyant chair!

Please note that owing to the present uncertain market in raw materials, the prices in this catalogue must be considered subject to fluctuation.

'Whiteleys famous furniture galleries', inter-war furniture catalogue.

Dramatic post-war cover design for Finmar with wood effect background.

One of the most admirable introductions appeared in a 1958 LINK catalogue, and should be used as compulsory reading for any design students who may have a tendency to prefer ego driven creativity to teamwork –

> Long before any piece of LINK furniture reaches the shop it goes through the most complex stages of design. Hundreds of drawings are considered – and scrapped. Dozens of prototypes are made. New woods, new veneers, new colours, new finishes are tried. Designers and craftsmen gather and discuss; experts and non-experts – just ordinary people who know what they want in future – test and talk and reject and start again.

After an introduction, a regular copy feature of catalogues would be a description and hype of the firm's hire purchase scheme, allaying fears, in advance, that the actually listed prices of the furniture could not be afforded. Hire purchase, which was to be a major factor in the expansion of the furniture industry, started as a somewhat shameful transaction to be kept secret as it suggested one's income fell short of one's ambitions.

But higher purchase was to morph, in the latter part of the 19th and into the 20th century, into a perfectly normal, even sensible, way to go about buying furniture. As early as the 18th century furnishers had offered, discreetly, terms to wealthy purchasers who were considered well able to meet the conditions of repayment. By the 1920s all the major furniture retailers were offering credit, although Shoolbred held out for a while with 'Ready money, no discounts'. Professor Peter Scott, in his research on the subject, estimated that by the mid-1920s some six million agreements were in place. To present their schemes in the best possible light, as something to be taken up without stigma, retailers came up with a very varied vocabulary – The Hackney Furnishing Co. in its catalogue called its scheme 'The Model System'; the Army & Navy Store and Whiteley's used 'deferred payments'; Bentall's as 'Easy Payments'; and Bowmans, devised one of the more positive descriptions – 'furnishing out of income'. Bolsom's similarly reassured potential customers that by its scheme there would be 'no need to endure weary months of saving'. The Hackney Furnishing Co.'s potential buyers might also have been reassured by its catalogue

declaration –

> If you are a poor man with only a few rooms
> you may have as much comfort in your home
> and as much beauty as the nobleman in his
> ancestral hall.

Maple and Gordon Russell, unusual bedfellows, but
in relation to hire purchase, linked by their stressing
of discretion, put out –

> Customers who do not wish to disturb their
> investments may avail themselves of these
> facilities. (Maples)

> We shall be glad to arrange terms of payment to
> suit customers special requirements.
> (Gordon Russell)

Such subtlety totally eluded Mr. Drage, the
showman, who blatantly had spread over one of his
catalogue's front cover –

> 50 Pay-Way
> means

Mr. & Mrs. Everyman talk things over with Mr. Drage

Mr. EVERYMAN: "What is this 50 Pay-Way, Mr. Drage?"
Mr. DRAGE: "50 Pay-Way means 50 Months to pay,
more than 4 years' Credit, and No Deposit. Thus for :—
   10/- you have £25 worth of furniture
   20/- you have £50 worth of furniture
   40/- you have £100 worth of furniture
and so on. And all the furniture delivered directly one
month's instalment is paid."

50 months to pay
and no deposit
– more than
4 years credit
Britain's best
Furnishing Terms

In addition to the pages devoted to hire purchase in its catalogues, Drage's put out a substantial booklet – 'The Drage 50 Pay-Way' in which a number of different types of people engage with Mr. Drage in discussions about their financial situations – from a mechanic to a clergyman, a railwayman to a doctor, he spread his net widely. Mr. Drage is even to be found responding to a somewhat coy Lady Secretary who timorously asks him 'can a business woman have these terms?' That Mr. Drage would be the epitomy of discretion was hinted by the description of these various discussions as 'delicate'. In its 1932 Xmas catalogue Drage's included an ingenious coloured cardboard wheel by which one indicated the amount one wished to spend and it then revealed the payments required under the Drage scheme.

Smart's also had a '4-year way' scheme and hyped it as 'Smart's famous credit terms', going all out to give hire purchase a positive image. In one of its catalogues, below a sketch of a Clark Gable look-a-like man with his head close to a Claudette Colbert look-a-like woman, Smart's has the husband gush –

As long as I live I'll remember the way Smart's made it possible for us to be so happy together. Their Easier to Pay – Smart's 4-Year Way solved all our problems – and didn't they treat us well darling!

Eventually the retailers' hard-sell for hire purchase rebounded with many of the smaller ones not having the capital to carry their schemes and either going out of business or being absorbed by the larger companies as The Times Furnishing Co. and the Great Universal Stores, by which time hire purchase had become a way of life.

When one comes on to the actual bulk of the furniture catalogues where products were illustrated and priced, copy writers again were used to extol their qualities. So frequently were certain adjectives used that their repetition must have

An interactive wheel to aid
purchasers considering hire
purchase, Drages.

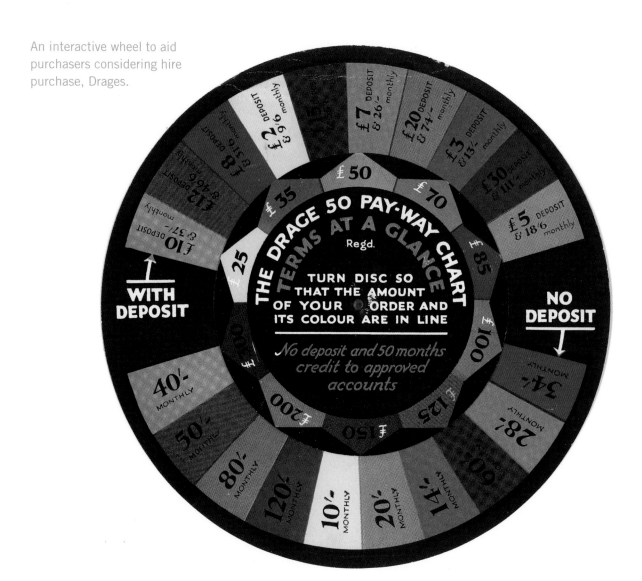

TUPPENCE PLAIN - PENNY COLOURED

numbed the discrimination of the reader – elegant, distinguished, charming, handsome, pleasant, graceful, pretty, luxurious, peaceful – the more 'masculine' adjectives being used for the study or library furniture, the more feminine for the bedroom suites.

A good many of the inter-war catalogues venerated the 'historic' as Maples's –

It will be no surprise therefore to find that the larger number of our best models have the artistic imprint of the well-known masters of the epoch – Chippendale, Sheraton, Hepplewhite, Shearer and others...

And the Times Furnishing Company's even more effusive –

Included in our enormous stock are designs taken from the finest periods in furniture history; the ornate Louis XV, the simplified and dignified Sheraton, the delicate Hepplewhite, and the perfectly proportioned Chippendale...

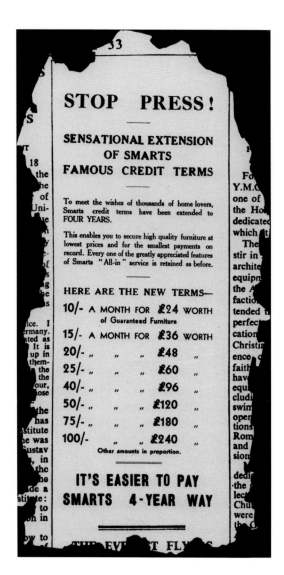

And even post-war, whilst other catalogues were stressing 'contemporary', Liberty was resorting to 'William and Mary', 'Jacobean', 'Adams' and 'Hathaway'.

Heal's and Gordon Russell, meanwhile, were promoting their wares by a variety of adjectives implying 'sensible' and 'good design' – Russell stressing 'solid' and 'clean lines', Heal's 'durable' and 'good proportions'. And it was the more 'design' orientated companies that did not merely list the woods used, but demonstrated a real respect and understanding of their materials. One Gordon Russell piece was 'built up in Honduras mahogany and veneered in Japanese chestnut and walnut rings' and another in 'English burr elm of a rich brown colour which blends specially well with the darker walnut'.

But perhaps of all descriptions given in furniture catalogues there can be few to reassure the reader more than that in an early Heal's issue for its iron and brass bedsteads – 'bed bugs and lice couldn't scale the slippery legs'!

In addition to any description and to a stock number, furniture would frequently be named, a custom that could as much have bewildered the would-be buyers as attracted them. For much of the naming, indeed for most of it, there seems no rhyme or reason, and it could well have been thought up on the spur of a moment by some unimaginative proprietor or copywriter noticing something out of the window, or thinking where they might go on holiday.

In fact, the most common names do seem to have been British towns of which Gates of Curtain Road appears to have had one of the longest lists, few of which bore any relevance at all to the furniture being sold, or even to where it was manufactured. Although one might have been attracted by pieces named 'Sandringham', 'Purley' and 'Essex' do not have quite the same pull; and one might have wondered at Gordon Russell's use of 'Aston', where there existed some of the worst slums of the time, albeit there were some dozen or so other more salubrious places with that name that Russell's may have had in mind; and would Waring's 'Norwood' suite have quite the same magnetism as its 'Henley'? The examples are endless – would Smart's 'Cambridge' have been preferred to Smart's 'Chelmsford', and so on, albeit Smart's did show some consistency of thought when it turned to the rich stream of rivers, possibly thinking it had exhausted suitable town names; there flowed out

THE OXFORD GROUP

A very choice Drawing Room Group, consisting of well-upholstered settee, two comfortable easy chairs and four small chairs with drop-in seats in charming tapestry, fancy table and choice cabinet. All mahogany finish.

7 PIECE SUITE	...	£17 - 0 - 0
TABLE	...	£1 - 12 - 0
CABINET	...	£3 - 18 - 0

GROUP COMPLETE £22 - 10 - 0
Any part can be supplied separately

DELIVERED ON PAYMENT OF ONLY 10!
10/- *monthly after*

DRAGES LTD · LONDON & BIRMINGHAM

THE SAVOY GROUP

A really charming dark Oak Dining Room Group. 5 ft. oak sideboard with three drawers (1 baize lined for cutlery) and two spacious cupboards. Draw-leaf dining table, extended 5 ft. by 3 ft., closed 3 ft. by 3 ft. Four small chairs and one carver chair with drop-in seats complete this very attractive group.

GROUP COMPLETE £33 - 10 - 0

DELIVERED ON PAYMENT OF ONLY 15!
15/- *monthly after*

DRAGES LTD · LONDON & BIRMINGHAM

'Usk', 'Medway', 'Tamar', Ribble', 'Shannon' and more.

Some companies set out to give their furniture 'class' as the Great Universal Stores with its three piece suites named 'Marquis' and 'Chancellor' and its chairs – 'Gladstone', 'General' and 'Emperor'; and even added a hint of culture with its 'Ruskin' bookshelf, although few of its customers might have understood the reference. And Smart's, along with its more common 'Chelmsford' and its rivers, resorted to what would immediately have

the connotation of luxury for its bedroom suites – 'Savoy', 'Ritz', 'Waldorf' and a string of similar hotels. And although these would have had a jazz age ring to them, Wolfe and Hollander went directly down the American route with its 'Klondyke' and 'Hollywood' pieces.

Very little of this naming, whether done by copy writers, production managers or sales people, related to the actual 'look' of the furniture, except, perhaps, for the 'historic' ranges. It wasn't really until Ernest Race, in the early post-war years, looked at his designs, with their spindly legs, saw a resemblance to similarly delicately legged creatures, and came up with Heron, Roebuck, Flamingo and Gazelle, although the link to Kangaroo is a little more tenuous.

Over the fifty years covered by this book, the furniture catalogue morphed from black and white or sepia to colour; from mere price lists to full-on productions; from selling of individual pieces to selling life-styles; from heavy tomes to light booklets and leaflets. Without any substantial market research evidence to validate the considerable financial outlay involved, furniture companies continued to have faith in the commercial effectiveness of a catalogue and continued to try to out-do competitors in the splendour or originality of their offerings. For social historians of domestic life, furniture catalogues will prove essential source documents; for those interested in graphic design they provide rather more meagre pickings.

DE-LUXE STATE ROOM

Q.S.T.S. QUEEN MARY

MAPLE LONDON

Correct Design
in Furniture at
London's Lowest Prices
Free Delivery by Motor
in 36 Counties

Above: Example of Maples advertising from 1925. **Opposite page:** Excerpt from advertisement for The Bath Cabinet Makers Co.

Apart from a few of the larger firms, furniture advertising in the 19th and early 20th centuries seems to have been mainly in the hands of the retailer and was mostly at a local level. A paper, such as the Hackney Gazette, which came out three times a week, regularly carried both Smart's and Jay's advertisements, local companies. Heal's and Maples were two of the earliest firms actually to make use of a broad range of media – newspapers, journals and hoardings – to get themselves and their wares better known. Heal's was placing its advertisements in national newspapers, as *The Times* and *The Herald*, by the mid-19th century. Maple, who had been advertising since the 1860s, had his considerable outpourings wryly commented upon in an article in *The Times* in 1903 – 'he (Maple) has continued to enlarge his borders to make his business well-known by advertisement'. Professor Peter Scott recorded that by the 1930s –

furniture advertising accounted for a higher proportion of total retail advertising than any other commodity group.

Few furniture companies had the ambition or the

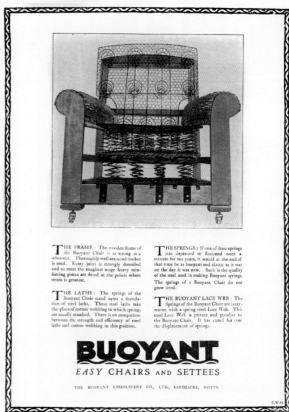

Above: Harrods advertisement, *Punch*, 1920. **Right:** 1922 advertisement for Buoyant Upholstery Co., *The Cabinet Maker and Complete House Furnisher*.

Opposite page: Two hoarding posters for The Times Furnishing Co. with space for the nearest shop address.

finance to use hoardings, although both Heal's and Maples did from time to time, Heal's are known to have taken advantage of hoardings on railway stations. But it was with the rapid expansion of the retail chain, the Times Furnishing Company, that 'outside' advertising was used to any extent by the industry. The Times Furnishing Co., in fact, made use of hoardings throughout the year, whilst only resorting to press advertising at what they considered crucial times in the market, Christmas and Easter. Its posters were changed as frequently as every four or five weeks to maintain as pristine an appearance as possible, given the normal wear and tear of street advertising. By the late 1930s the company was spending as much as £15,000 a year on its outside advertising, much of this going on the actual rental of sites. The company described its press advertising as its 'heavy guns', its posters as its 'infantry', to be used for local appeal as usually

carrying a space for the address of the nearest branch in the vicinity.

One example of the Times Furnishing Company's ingenuity with the poster was when, in 1938, they made use of the escalators at Holborn underground station. Passengers using the 'up' escalator passed three of its posters, in a sequence –

'Turn Right'
'Turn Right Again'
'To the Times Furnishing Co.'

Between the top of the escalator and the booking office was additionally mounted a large map showing all the company's London branches and how to get there by underground.

When it came to press advertising the same

opportunities were open to the furniture industry as to those for other commodities – trade journals, magazines and newspapers. The main trade journals for the furnishing industry were *The Cabinet Maker and Complete House Furnisher* (published every Friday), the *Furniture Record and the Furnisher*, the *Furnishing Trades' Organiser*, *Furnishing*, *Furnishing World* and the *Furniture Record World*. Targeted at the industry these largely carried advertisements of suppliers to the industry, as sellers of glues, veneers, upholstery and such, but all carried advertisements of furniture manufacturers as well. The copy in these publications was mainly on technical, business and professional matters and news relating to the industry. A typical example was the Furnishing Trade's Organiser carrying, in the 20s, numbers of furniture advertisements, some of them coloured, for the likes of Drages, as well as general trade articles and others commissioned from key personalities of the time as Ambrose Heal and Sir Samuel Waring.

Women were probably key to the actual choosing of furniture to be bought, although, at the period, probably less frequently the actual payers of the

bill, yet 'women's' magazines, as such, tended to be preoccupied with matters of beauty, fashion, cookery, health and motherhood. If furniture advertisements appeared at all in this section of the press they would be almost entirely related to furnishing the kitchen. The bulk of furniture advertising in magazines occurred in 'house' publications, which proliferated in the inter-war years – *Household Words, Home, Home Chat, Home Companion, Home Notes, House Beautiful, Ideal Home, Homes & Gardens* and the like. Occasionally a few of the larger companies, with bigger budgets, would use general interest magazines as 'Punch', 'The Spectator' and 'The Illustrated London News'.

There was a small, elite section of the press, in the inter-war years, that was specifically concerned with 'design' – journals that both carried furniture advertisements and had editorials and articles hyping 'good' furniture design. These tended to have a select readership of architects, interior designers and the like, and seem to have been largely preaching to the converted. Nevertheless they would have had some influence, particularly

1920s *Ideal Home* magazine cover.

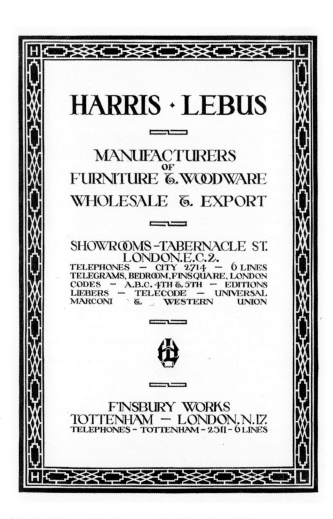

Harris Lebus advertisement in *The Furnishing Trades' Organiser*, undated.

on the contract furnishing market, say for offices, hotels and ships. The most enduring of these was The Studio's annual *Decorative Art*, which ran in the inter-war years and took up the cause of 'modernism' in a big way, extolling the trend towards –

> ...greater simplicity and restraint, a reaction, no doubt, against the unwholesome stuffiness of the Victorian home with its musty atmosphere of a third-rate museum.

Design orientated companies as Gordon Russell's, Green & Abbott, Bowmans, and latterly Pel, placed advertisements in the annual, and were frequently hyped by it. *Modern Publicity*, another annual issued by The Studio, did not carry furniture advertisements as such, but would give examples of furniture advertisements if they were sufficiently noteworthy. Few were, in fact, selected as outstanding, either by *Modern Publicity* or by the major design monthly running through the fifty years covered by this book – *Commercial Art* (later retitled *Art & Industry* and, finally, *Design for Industry*).

Designers in Britain was a prestigious publication that came out intermittently between 1947 and 1971 (seven issues in all), in which the Society of Industrial Artists offered a review of the best designs of the time to help manufacturers, publishers and advertisers who were considering commissioning artists. The bulky volumes carried advertisements at the back, and Heal's, Dunn's, and Morris of Glasgow all appeared over the years. A typical selection of furniture designers featuring in the review section was that given in the 1951 issue – Scottish Furniture Manufacturers, Scottish Co-operative Wholesale Society, Primavera, Hille, Dunn's, Heal's, Liberty, Gordon Russell, H.K. Furniture, Ernest Race Ltd., along with art college students' work.

Post-war, however, with the establishment of the Council of Industrial Design, its journal *Design* did carry a regular feature – 'Furniture Survey', initially written by A. Gardner Medwin of the Council. In the 50s and 60s Heal's was one of the few 'oldtimers' to still be in the limelight, mentioned in it, along with the relatively new boys on the block – Hille (under the Julius's), Ernest Race, Pegram,

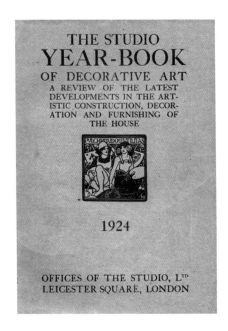

THE STUDIO
YEAR-BOOK
OF DECORATIVE ART
A REVIEW OF THE LATEST
DEVELOPMENTS IN THE ART-
ISTIC CONSTRUCTION, DECOR-
ATION AND FURNISHING OF
THE HOUSE

1924

OFFICES OF THE STUDIO, Lᵀᴰ
LEICESTER SQUARE, LONDON

Oak Unit furniture, designed and hand-made here.
No. 8 2ft. Oak Bureau £6. 19. 6. Nos. 7 and 7a
Cupboard Bookcases, 2ft. 9in. wide, each £4.15.0
List showing Units for all rooms post free

p·e·gane LTD
FURNITURE AND CARPETS
COLLEGE GREEN BRISTOL

A DE-LUXE STATE ROOM   Q.S.T.S. QUEEN MARY

THE BATH CABINET MAKERS
COMPANY, LIMITED, BATH
MAKERS OF FINE CONTEMPORARY AND TRADITIONAL
FURNITURE, ARCHITECTURAL DECORATION, PANEL-
LING, PLASTERWORK, SHOP FITTINGS, BANK FITTINGS.
THE BATH CABINET MAKERS CO. LTD. BATH, ENGLAND
PHONE: BATH 7214-7215.   GRAMS, ART, BATH
LONDON SHOWROOM 4 CAVENDISH SQUARE, W.I
PHONE AND GRAMS - LANGHAM - 2860.

Meredew, Dunn's (under Geoffrey), Primavera, and Conran.

Although furniture advertising made little mark when it came to graphic design, some of the larger firms did in fact begin to try to make their advertising more professional by using advertising agencies, particularly when they were planning to launch a new range, for which they realized they lacked the relevant resources – examples are Bowmans using Stuart's, Lusty's turning to Royds, Smart's retaining Greenley's, Buouyant going with Charles W. Hobson, Heal's working with Pritchard Wood, Gomme's with J. Walter Thompson and Parker-Knoll with Vernon's.

In the inter-war years Smart's along with Greenley's made some stir with a series of advertisements in story format. Greenley noted of furniture buying –

> There is always a new problem to be solved, a new story to be told, always of fresh interest to the reader.

A typical Greenley's 'story' would be that of a young man at last finding a suitable flat but not knowing where to start in furnishing it.

Two examples when advertising agents were brought in for new product launches were Parker's bringing in Vernon's for the launch of Parker-Knoll, and Gomme's using J. Walter Thompson for its G-Plan. It wasn't so much Parker-Knoll bringing in Vernon's but the reverse. One of Vernon's employees noticed what he considered a rather pathetic initial advertisement for the Parker-Knoll sprung chair and as a result Vernon's took the initiative and approached the company. Vernon's were the first advertising agency that Parker-Knoll used and their relationship was to continue for some fifty years from 1932 onwards. Parker-Knoll were lucky to have such design orientated directors as Thomas Parker and Geoffrey Alpe, who not only influenced the design of its furniture but of its advertising. Vernon's, on its side, became much more than an ideas associate, but actually influenced the way the company operated, as when it suggested the usefulness of factory quality testing so that a five-year guarantee could be offered when furniture

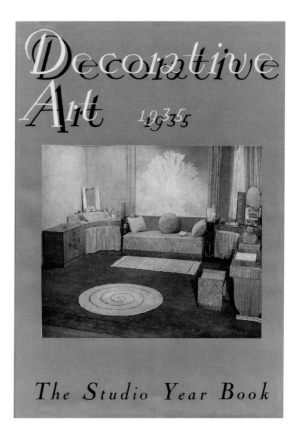

Cover of *Decorative Art*, 1935.

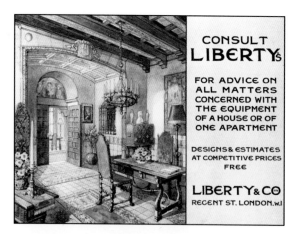

The 'Bickley' chair, designed by Geoffrey Dunn and Maurice Russell, A.R.I.B.A.

Top: Liberty advertisement – still offering their baronial style – from *Decorative Art*, 1933.
Above: Dunn's of Bromley advert from *Designers in Britain*, 1951.

was bought and this advantage made much of in advertisements. Parker-Knoll was to produce some of the most colourful furniture advertisements in the post-war years in the national press, in magazines and in provincial newspapers.

J. Walter Thompson's was key to Gomme's launch of its 'G-Plan' range. The campaign is noteworthy not only because of the extensiveness of the advertising used, but because women were involved – a rarity in the furniture trade, Hille being a major exception. It was Doris Gundry, of the agency, who coined 'G-Plan', and an agency artist, one Petronella Hodges, who designed some of the advertisements. With Hille, although Robin Day had been responsible for much of its graphic as well as its furniture design, the mantel was taken over later on by Rosamind Julius, Ray and Maurice's daughter, who became responsible for much of their stationery and promotions design.

Copy for furniture advertisements was as varied as that for any other product, from Gomme's G-Plan advertisements, where a page of illustration had an accompanying full page of copy, to McIntosh's

20th CENTURY FURNITURE

should be furniture designed for contemporary needs, using all contemporary materials and all the advantages of modern machines and tools.

Such furniture is made at the Russell Workshops, Broadway, Worcs. and is illustrated in Russell Catalogues and Lists for which you are invited to write.

BROADWAY
WORCESTERSHIRE

London Showrooms
28, WIGMORE ST.
W. I.

Rosewood veneered and walnut dining table. Cherrywood dining chairs.

GORDON RUSSELL
LTD.

AD. III

Made on a completely new principle of construction, derived from experimental work on Mosquito fuselages and the manufacture of helicopter blades during the war, this prize-winning dining room chair was specially designed for Morris of Glasgow by Basil Spence, O.B.E., F.R.I.B.A. It is made of over a hundred laminations of Honduras mahogany and Canadian betula bonded together under high frequency electrical and hydraulic pressure with pheno-formaldehyde resin adhesive. This chair is part of the "Allegro" dining room suite, comprising elliptical dining table, six chairs and a sideboard, is now available to the public. Selected for exhibition by the American Architectural League, it is now a permanent exhibit in the Museum of Modern Art in New York.

MORRIS of GLASGOW
makers of fine furniture

H. MORRIS & CO. LTD., MILTON STREET, GLASGOW, C.4

Full page Gordon Russell advertisement, *The Studio Year-Book of Decorative Art*, 1931.

Morris of Glasgow advertisement in *Designers in Britain*, 1949.

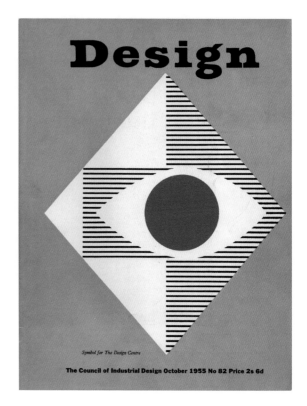

Symbol for The Design Centre

The Council of Industrial Design October 1955 No 82 Price 2s 6d

Left: Early publication of the CoID. **Above:** Cover of *Design*, the magazine of the CoID.

advertisement where one piece of furniture had as copy just 'furniture by McIntosh', or Race's Heron chair advertisement where just a photo of the chair with its stool had no copy whatsoever, just, in small letters at the bottom, the name Race; or Morris of Glasgow's advertisements during the Festival of Britain which were all copy with not a glimpse of a piece of furniture. Few would have read through the dense text of the G-Plan advertisement but their eye may well have been drawn, in relief, to the relatively blank rectangle encouraging readers to write for a catalogue.

Of course hype was to be found across the board, and furniture was no exception, with Maples selling itself as 'the largest furniture house in the world', Parker-Knoll's boasting 'England's best selling chair', Oetzmann's claiming to help make 'Homes of Distinction', and Hampton's asserting the reputation it had held 'for more than a hundred years'. But furniture, presumably because of its relative expense, would also make much use of the concept 'value for money', examples being Arding & Hobb's 'From the House of Good Value', Heal's 'Where lovely things cost less than you expect', Maples

'Correct design in furniture at London's Lowest prices' and Bowmans 'the first firm to sell good modern design at reasonable prices'.

'Modern' was a word much used in furniture advertising in the inter-war years when so much furniture being sold was of the historic reproduction kind. Heal's had its 'modern tendencies', Whiteley's its 'modern living' and Fortnum & Mason, accompanying the illustration of a glass covered table, 'modernity is mirrored in our furniture'. Other firms, held on to a thread of traditional whilst suggesting that they were as 'with it' as any, hoping thus to net as wide a spread of buyers as possible, as Hampton's 'modernity with dignity', Gordon Russell's 'respects tradition without aping antique styles', and Parker-Knoll's more expansive 'the design reflects the mid-18th century but the comfort is strictly to-day'. In the post-war years the word 'contemporary' took over from 'modernity', which by then had been fairly well accepted as integral to much design.

Of course furniture being expensive and in constant use it was important for advertisements to convey

Are you enjoying the Festival? The boat you came in, the house or hotel you are living in and the Festival Bar in which you take your aperitif — one or all of these may have been furnished by*

MORRIS OF GLASGOW

Cumbrae furniture is worth taking home as a Souvenir

Write to 147 Milton Street, Glasgow for the current Morris magazine. Offices also at the Building Centre, Brunswick Place, Leeds, and with Charles McNeil, 3 St. James's Place, London, S.W.1.

＊ We have made aircraft parts too !

Fine furniture

by

Morris of Glasgow

You are invited to write for a copy of the current MORRIS MAGAZINE

H. MORRIS & CO., LTD., MILTON STREET, GLASGOW, C4

the idea of durability. Heal's tended to use the adjective 'sound', Conran's for its contract work the more slangy 'tough', whilst Lloyd Loom combined 'comfort and durablitity'. Few advertisers ventured far into detailing the actual technical construction of their products, but Parker-Knoll showed some originality with its 'you can't go shopping with a penknife to see what's underneath when buying upholstery'. Perhaps Ercol produced one of the most poetic advertising offerings including elements of functionality and, could it be said, just the merest touch of humour, when launching a new range in 1956 –

> Chairs that welcome you with open arms, dining chairs to feast your eyes on, a love seat you will love at first sight, settees to settle down in, even a stool to put your feet up on.

Curiously furniture advertising made little use, in its copy, of testimonials, references from the 'great and good', so frequently used by other product advertisers, particularly for health products; nor did it make the most of major events and celebrations, royal or otherwise, that proved such rich pickings

Above: Heal's advert emphasizing functional design, or 'sound' furniture, 1928.
Opposite page: A pair of advertisements for Morris of Glasgow, with one (far left) without a sight of furniture, both 1951.

elsewhere, as for car and petrol advertising. One very rare and, indeed, humorous example, was Sebel Products using the name and image of Tessie O'Shea, a music hall entertainer known as two-ton Tessie, thus implying the sturdiness of its garden chairs if they could take her weight! A few companies as Race and Nathan's linked their products with the Festival of Britain, but other examples are scarce.

Perhaps one of the most lengthy and certainly the most odd furniture advertising copy, making use of Napoleon's name, was Parker-Knoll's illustration of a chair with an inset photograph of a good-looking young woman –

> Miss Weston stays at home – and already two of the nicest young men have implored her to go out. As a matter of fact, Miss Weston's employer has just read a life of Napoleon, and when at seven-thirty with a fine sense of pageantry he took a cab for Waterloo, Miss Weston, poor thing, was a nervous wreck. Now more than ever she thanks heaven (and a generous great-aunt) for her new Parker-Knoll.

the Heron chair　　and foot stool

RACE FURNITURE · LONDON

MODERNITY IS MIRRORED

IN OUR FURNITURE AND FABRICS

Our collection of mirror furniture truly reflects the spirit of the new fashion. Sophisticatedly modern, with the dignity of extreme simplicity, it is very individual and distinctive. Our fabrics, too, are more than experiments in Beauty. We have a very large collection entirely exclusive to ourselves, designed and planned by the expert hand and eye, to suit your personal taste

FORTNUM AND MASON

2nd Floor · Piccadilly · London

REGent 8040

AD. VIII

Unpick that one!

Beyond the copy there is the 'look' of furniture advertising to consider. For readers interested in either the history of advertising or the history of graphic design, furniture advertisements do not immediately come to mind, in fact may have fallen completely below their radar. Where, they may ask, are the images to match those of McKnight Kauffer, Tom Eckersley or Hans Schleger; where is the typography of the likes of Ashley Havinden or the whimsy of Edward Bawden. It is perhaps paradoxical that although the British furniture industry produced iconic designers in the 20th century, as Gordon and Dick Russell, Ambrose and Christopher Heal, Robin Day and Ernest Race, as a subject, furniture seems largely to have failed to ignite the creative enthusiasm of the graphic designers of the period.

Much of furniture illustration for advertisements, certainly early on, would have been done in-house or at a local printers, and would be in black and white – drawings, etchings, scraperboard and very rarely the odd water colour. Colour photography was only in full flood for furniture advertisements after WWII by which time everyone had taken it up – Ercol, Meredew, Greaves & Thomas, Cintique, Maple, Gomme, Stag, and so on; although some firms, as Maples, Harrods and Morris of Glasgow still seem to have made much use of line drawings.

Lusty's, holding the British patent for Lloyd Loom furniture, were lucky in that its furniture was made of screwed paper in a wide range of colours, so that its advertisements stood out from the others in the inter-war period. Lusty's had a different image problem in that its furniture was largely seen as suitable for the garden. It turned to Royd's advertising agency, George Royd reporting his brief being to visually 'bring our furniture into the home'. This Royd's achieved by initially giving its artwork dreamy colours and setting it in ambiguous surroundings so that it was not at all clear whether it was outdoors or in. Gradually in its visuals, Royd's moved the furniture inwards and presented it as of use the whole year round, in house and garden, not just for the garden in summer.

Above: Rare use of humour in furniture advertising, Sebel, undated. **Opposite page:** Fortnum and Mason advert, 1935.

A Lounge in the modern style—furnished by Oetzmann

HOMES OF DISTINCTION

For a century past, Oetzmann's have specialized in the complete furnishing and equipment of the home, in all periods and styles.

It is part of the Oetzmann Service to devise furnishing schemes that attain a delightful and artistic effect at a moderate cost. It is only necessary for customers to indicate generally what is required.

Oetzmann's staff are always ready with advice and suggestions. Their knowledge and judgment is freely offered whether the purchase concerns a single piece or the furnishing of an entire home.

(OETZMANN AND COMPANY LTD.)
67-87 HAMPSTEAD ROAD, LONDON, N.W.1   EUSton 3000

Above: Oetzmann advertisement, undated.
Opposite page: Excerpt from a 1968 advertisement for Parker-Knoll, note the rare use of sex appeal.

Although furniture advertising eventually adopted colour in a big way, it never understood the attraction of visual humour, particularly that of the kind of English whimsy that the likes of Shell and Fortnum & Mason had used to such advantage. And if humour was lacking, so were people! Sideboard drawers need to be opened smoothly, armchairs shown to fit the skeleton, desks to be high and stable for elbows, and so on. Yet until after WWII people were rarely to be seen in furniture advertisements, except for the kitchen where they would be mainly demonstrating the latest equipment. When most other inter-war advertisements were thronging with people – men-about-town smoking, drinking the choicest wines, women besporting the complicated contraptions of corsets or demonstrating the freedom of sportswear, families crouched round a radio set or an early television, or driving into the countryside in the latest Austin – furniture advertising was largely peopleless. And more, furniture advertisers seem to have been totally unaware of sex appeal, which for eons had not only sold fashion and beauty products but cars and a myriad of other not obviously sex-related products. When women began to feature

in furniture advertisements, perched on the end of beds or sitting on the edge of couches, they are largely posed stiltedly, Parker-Knolls perhaps having the first woman actually snuggling into a chair. When men and women appeared, even in the early post-WWII years, the woman could well be placed on the couch with the man a distance away in an armchair. The conservative furniture trade, at least for the period of this book, just did not catch on to the fact that sex had its commercial rewards, so to speak!

But what some of the furniture trade did catch on to was the importance of the repetition of some kind of trademark, symbol, emblem or other device by which a company's messages, put over by whatever media – when driving past a hoarding, thumbing through a magazine – could be immediately recognized. The device could be merely initials which had been found to be so successful elsewhere, as with RR, or P&O, or DAKS; or it could be an object as the scallop shell of the Shell Oil Company; or a cute figure as Mr. Therm for the gas industry or Guiness's Toucan. Furniture companies were not slow in registering trademarks for themselves and brand symbols for their products, Heal's being one of the earliest with its 'sign of the four poster'.

Although few firms had the confidence to use initials from the start, as did Pel (altogether more snappy than Practical Equipment Company), others eventually caught on to the idea, as Nathan's use of 'N' (with echoes of things Napoleonic), McIntosh of Kirkready using just 'Mc' and Gomme's using 'G-Plan'. A few came to use distinctive typography, with the early lead of The Times Furnishing Co. (plagiarizing the newspaper font). Post-war, a number of the more design-orientated companies developed their own typography, including Cintique, Hille (with its elongated lettering), Conran, Race and the curious, but nevertheless immediately recognizable, Greaves & Thomas enlargened ampersand. Perhaps the most frequently used initials, although few would have understood them as such, was with the mark for the government's WWII utility scheme. The strong two Cs, devised by removing wedges from two circles, followed by 41, actually stood for Controlled Commodity, and

appeared on all products meeting the government's austerity standards for some ten years on from 1941. It is one of the few symbols whose designer's name is known, one Reginald Shipp, who was working at the time for Hargreaves, a company which supplied manufacturing labels and whose submitted design won out over others who had been invited to compete. Shipp was awarded £5 for his creative solution!

Cute figures, animals and people were less common in furniture advertisements than in those for other products, an exception being Stag using the obvious for its advertisements. The nearest to the likes of Mr. Therm was Ercol's lion, which first appeared in silhouette as a trademark as early as 1928 (thought to have been adopted as a symbol of 'sturdiness' as characteristic of the lions in Trafalgar Square), but soon to appear in much of the firm's advertising, frisking around in his craftsman's apron, befurnished with woodworker's tools. The craft origin of the furniture trade was also used as a trademark by Gordon Russell's with its circular saw; and a further example of a craft-related device was Parker-Knoll's ingenious 'man on a spring' with the

A selection of furniture logos.

Further selection of furniture logos.

tag 'tension suspension', created by James Fitton, the Art Director of Vernon's.

Although the advertisements of many furniture firms became familiar because of these various devices, few were able to make use of the device that carried the greatest kudos – the Royal Warrant, possibly because most royal residences were in fact furnished with antique inherited furniture. The two early exceptions were Maple and Heal's, both of which were to receive the warrant in the 1880s and make use of it from time to time in their advertisements; later Wylie & Lochhead were similarly recognized. In terms of snobbery a lesser recognition of worth, albeit in design spheres an altogether more valid recognition of standards achieved was the post-war Council of Industrial Design labelling scheme, which would also occasionally be used in advertisements.

Heal's as one of the longest lasting furniture firms provides interesting examples of how furniture advertising evolved over the fifty years of this book. Heal's earliest convention was to border its advertisements, which made them easily

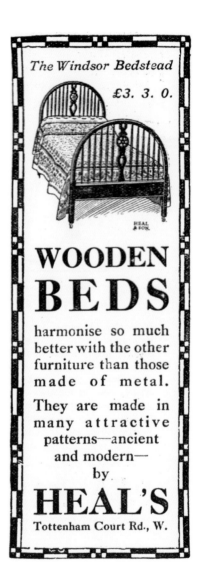

The Windsor Bedstead
£3. 3. 0.

WOODEN BEDS

harmonise so much better with the other furniture than those made of metal.

They are made in many attractive patterns—ancient and modern—by

HEAL'S
Tottenham Court Rd., W.

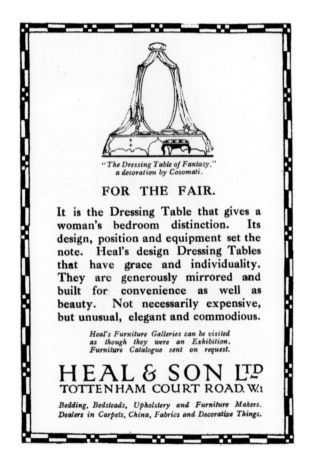

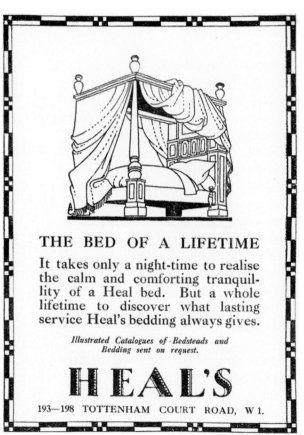

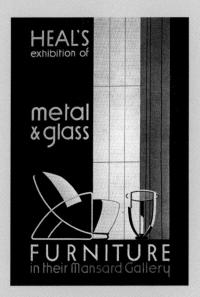

ENGLISH CHARACTER

Furniture, as simple as this, has, of necessity, to be well and truly made. The limed Canadian pine has fine figure and a warm grey tone, which derives subtle emphasis from the darker yew-tree handles. The horizontal mouldings are appropriately reticent and have a quiet dignity. The price, in keeping with the design, is modest and reasonable.

HEAL'S

HEAL & SON LTD · 196 TOTTENHAM COURT ROAD · LONDON · W1

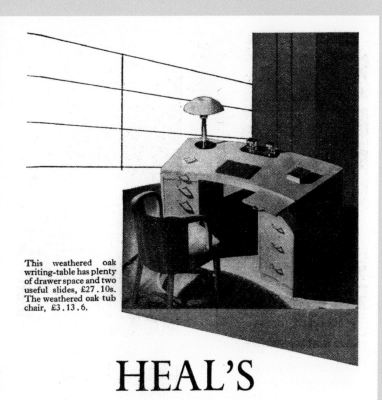

This weathered oak writing-table has plenty of drawer space and two useful slides, £27.10s. The weathered oak tub chair, £3.13.6.

HEAL'S

Where lovely things

cost less than you expect

HEAL & SON LTD · 196 TOTTENHAM COURT ROAD · W1

First impressions *last*

Does your reception room give visitors the right idea of your company's character and outlook? Or is it a dignified but dull relic of an earlier day? Remember, first impressions not only count – they *last*. This reception room in a well-known London Advertising Agency was recently refurbished by Heal's. If you would like to see some more of our ideas for individual offices, boardrooms, hotels and ships, tell your secretary to write for *Furniture for Special Needs*.

HEAL'S CONTRACTS LTD

196 TOTTENHAM COURT ROAD, LONDON, W.1.   Telephone : Museum 1666

Contemporary Furniture

A large selection of both utility and fine hand-made furniture of good design can be seen in our showrooms. If you are unable to call, we will gladly send you a copy of our folder "Contemporary Furniture at Heal's". Deferred payments can be arranged.

★ **The Restaurant is open for morning coffee, lunch and tea. Fully licensed.**

HEAL & SON

HEAL'S UTILITY BEDROOM FURNITURE IN LIGHT OAK. *Also in London Plane Tree or Australian Walnut, designed by Christopher Heal, M.S.I.A.* Three pieces—wardrobe 4 ft. wide ; dressing table, six drawers and adjustable mirror ; cupboard chest, 2 ft. 9 ins. wide—£75.12.3. The following pieces to match are also available:—Dwarf wardrobe, 2 ft. 9 ins. wide £19.6.9.; Writing-toilet table £22.12.0.; Bedside table £4.4.0.; Bedside cupboard £5.4.0.; Dressing chair £2.15.0.; Bedstead, 3 ft. wide £8.12.0.; 4 ft. 6 ins. wide £10.18.9.

HEAL & SON LTD., 196 TOTTENHAM COURT ROAD, W.1,   TELEPHONE: MUSEUM 1666

recognizable. A 1927 advertisement was handled by The London Press Exchange – an early example of a furniture company using an advertising agency. The illustration was by Aldo Cosomati, a very popular commercial artist of the time. A Heal's 1930s advertisement shows its leap into 'modernity' with particularly good typography. Its 1935 'English Character' advertisement demonstrates in its copy Heal's continual concern for materials and design, and this, and its *Punch* advertisement of 1938 emphasise the company's desire to produce good design at 'reasonable' prices, educating as wide a public as possible. Heal's use of the word

'contemporary' in its Ideal Home advertisement in 1951 means exactly that, as the government's Utility Furniture Scheme was still in operation. Some of the firm's most interesting advertising was when it was expanding its contract business in the post-war years. By the 1950s Heal's was retaining Pritchard Wood & Ptnrs. as its agent, with John Gloag as its contact executive, and this seems to have raised its standard for advertising design which brought it to the attention of *Modern Publicity* – a rarity for the furniture trade. The 1964 advertisement shows Heal's still up with the best in terms of the design of its advertisements – layout, copy and visuals.

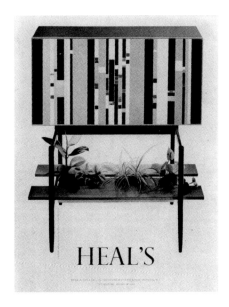

From left to right: 'First impressions *last*', *Ideal Home*, 1951; 'Contemporary Furniture', *Design*, 1951; 'Heal's', *Modern Publicity*, 1957–8; 'A new approach to sitting down', *Good Housekeeping*, 1964.

a new approach to sitting down

The head-over-Heal's feeling is confusing me. Here are all these wonderful new chairs, and I don't know whether to sit in them now or rush them home in a taxi. There's always something going on at Heal's; always something to see. Six floors full of the world's best in home-making design. Go right round Europe, you won't find a shop with so many beautiful things for your home, so much practical knowledge of fine design. Heal's in Tottenham Court Road is Europe's most exciting furniture shop. **For that can't-wait-to-get-it-home feeling...**

HEAL'S
Europe's most exciting furniture shop

K43 Sink in, settle down, swivel round – so comfortable in Arne Dahlen's 'Juliet' upholstered chair. From – £28.15.0 | K8133. Modern rocking chair from Denmark; in beech with natural finish, or painted black or white. From – £23.10.0 | K8134. An essay in simplicity – superbly simple Danish teak chair, with smooth, smartly covered seat. £18.10.0

These chairs are all from Heal's Cont/ex collection of exclusive imported furniture.

Heal & Son Limited 196 Tottenham Court Road London W1   Museum 1666.   Buses 1, 14, 24, 29 39, 73, 127, 134, 156, 176 or Goodge Street Underground. Customers' Underground Car Park

Fold-out promotional booklet for Dunn's of Bromley.

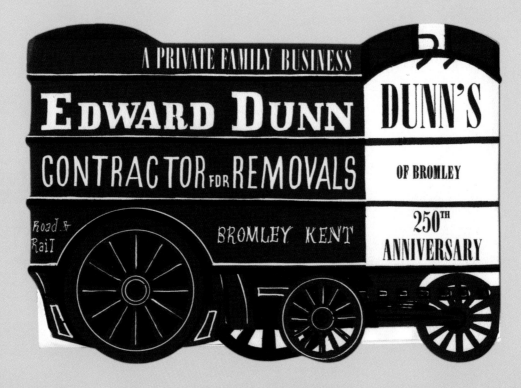

TUPPENCE PLAIN - PENNY COLOURED

Epilogue

The years covered by this book, 1920 to 1970, saw mergers and takeovers in the furniture industry. Selling became a matter for large conglomerates and furniture chains, some owned by cynical finance people, far removed from the aspiring craftspeople, designers and shopkeepers who had originally started up their businesses in small workshops, studios and single-fronted shops. A few courageous, some would say foolish, evangelicals, dotted across London and beyond, for a time carried the flag of 'good' design, but sooner or later were obliged to give up the good fight. Even Conran, the democratiser of furniture selling with Habitat, had some rather shaky moments in our time period.

And then came a teenager, one Ingvar Kamprad, who grew up on a farm called Elmtaryd, in a town called Agunnaryd, in southern Sweden (thus IKEA). What would Blundell Maple or Ambrose Heal, Harris Lebus or Benjamin Drage have made

of hundreds, sometimes thousands of citizens, queuing orderly, within barriers, as if cattle come to market, on a Sunday morning, waiting for a furniture store to open; and then being prepared to be guided in an orderly fashion through the various departments and obediently to tick off the goods they had selected (and may well not have had in mind earlier that Sunday); and, further, visiting the warehouse section and personally piling goods on to trolleys, to yet again queue patiently at the check-outs. IKEA came to Britain in 1987. The buying and selling of furniture, its buildings, its catalogues, its advertising and publicity, would never be the same again.

But that is another story.

Bibliography

BIBLIOGRAPHY

1937 Nikolaus Pevsner, *An Enquiry into Industrial Art in England*, Cambridge University Press.

1951 *The Anatomy of Design*, Royal College of Art.

1955 Michael Farr, *Design in British Industry: A mid-century survey*, Cambridge University Press.

1969 David Joel, *Furniture Design Set Free*, J.M. Dent & Sons.

1974 Geffrye Museum catalogue, *Utility Furniture and Fashion: 1941–1951*, Inner London Educational Authority.

1981 Sutherland Lyall, *Hille: 75 years of British Furniture*, Elron Press Ltd.

1982 Hazel Conway, *Ernest Race*, The Design Council.

1985 Raymond Plummer, *Nothing need be ugly*, DIA.

1987 Pat Kirkham et al, *Furnishing the World: the East London Furniture Trade 1830–1980*, Journeyman.

1991 Lee J. Curtis, *Lloyd Loom woven fabric furniture*, Salamander Books.

1992 Hugh Barty-King, *Maples Fine Furnishers: A Household Name for 150 Years*, Quiller Press.

1992 Jeremy Myerson, *Gordon Russell, designer of furniture 1892–1992*, Design Council/Gordon Russell Ltd.

1997 William I. Massil, *Immigrant Furniture Workers in London 1881–1939*, The Jewish Museum/The Geffrye Museum.

1999 ed. Judy Attfield, *Utility reassessed: the role of ethics in the practice of design*, Manchester University Press.

2000 David Jeremiah, *Architecture and Design for the Family in Britain, 1900–1970*, Manchester University Press.

2001 Lesley Jackson, *Robin & Lucienne Day: pioneers of contemporary design*, Mitchell Beazley.

2006 Smith & Rogers, *Behind the Veneer*, English Heritage.

2007 Prof. Peter Scott, *Mr. Drage, Mr Everyman, and the creation of a mass market for domestic furniture in inter-war Britain*, University of Reading.

2007 Basil Hyman and Steven Braggs, *The G-Plan Revolution*, Booth-Clibborn Editions.

2008 Jon Mills, *Utility Furniture* – the 1943 Utility Furniture Catalogue with an explanation of Britain's Second World War Utility Furniture Scheme, Sabrestorm Publishing.

2011 C. Edwards, *Tottenham Court Road: the changing fortunes of London's furniture street 1850–1950*, Loughborough University.

2013 Lesley Jackson, *Ercol: Furniture in the Making*, Richard Denis.

2013 Lesley Jackson, *Modern British Furniture Design since 1945*, V&A Publishing.

2014 Ruth Artmonsky, *Exhibiting Ourselves*, Artmonsky Arts.

Drage Way

My name is Mr. Everyman, I'm married it is true.
I only married recently because I'd no work to do.
The moment I got married my wife started in to grouse,
for in my haste I hadn't thought of looking for a house.
So we got one out at Golder's Green, we looked on at the outside.
Till I discovered we shall want some furniture inside.
Well I hadn't any money, so my wife flew in a rage,
So there was nothing for it, so I went to Mr. Drage.
So off we went to Drage's just as quickly as could be.
Mr. Drage was very nice, he turned and said to me,
'Good Morning Mr. Everyman, what can I do for you?'
I said, 'It's rather awkward Mr. Drage what shall I do?
For see we've only just got married and I'm on the rocks and broke'.
He said, 'Don't let that worry you, why money is a joke.
We only run our business to oblige you sort of folk,
And we always lay your lino on the floor.'

So I said, 'Well that's splendid, but no references have I got'.
He said, 'We don't want them, they're a lot of tommy rot,
Why you needn't give your name if you rather not,
And we always lay your lino on the floor'.
£500 in furniture she spent, did my old Dutch.
'What deposit Mr. Drage,' I said, 'would you require for such?'
He simply smiled and said, 'Would two and sixpence be too much?
And we always lay the lino on your floor.'

Music hall song, lyrics by Clarkson Rose

So I said, 'Two and sixpence Mr. Drage, you're very kind.'
'Now what about instalments?' he said, 'that's as you're inclined,
say half-a-crown a year, and if you can't well never mind,
and we always lay your lino on the floor'.
The I said, 'Mr. Drage, suppose I'm taken ill,
And cannot keep the payments up?' He said, 'it costs you nil.
We keep you while you're out of work and pay your doctor's bill,
And we always lay your lino on the floor.'
Then I said, 'The neighbours in our road are bound to know we're new,
And when they see your van they're bound to say a thing or two'.
He said, 'They wont, we send your stuff in vans as plain as you,
And we always lay your lino on the floor.'
And he said, 'From today our special policy begins,
Insuring you for burglary and fire and double chins.
It pays for you a thousand pounds if you should click for twins,
And still we lay the lino on the floor.'

The I said, 'Goodbye and thank you Mr. Drage, you've been most fair,'
And he said, 'Good morning Mr. Everyman and I declare.'
My wife said, 'Mr. Drage you wont forget our railway fare,
When you send to lay the lino on the floor.'
D D Drages, beautiful Drages,
that's the place to furnish if you're poor.
Be it ever so humble, or be it a mansion,
Well they always lay your lino on the floor!